Don't Look Down

An Adventurous Life with MS

ROGER CHISHOLM

Scotland Street Press

Published by Scotland Street Press 2017

First published in Scotland in 2017 by
Scotland Street Press
scotlandstreetpress@gmail.com

ISBN: 978-1-910895-20-7

Typeset by Hewer Text UK LTd, Edinburgh
Printed and bound in Poland

Cover photographs by Howard Steen

Pervixi: neque enim fortuna malignior unquam
eripiet nobis quod prior hora dedit
(Petronius).

I have lived; nor shall maligner fortune ever
take from me what an earlier hour once gave.
(as translated by Aldous Huxley).

This book is dedicated to my dear children Elinor and Owen, and to my very good friends Peter and Howard. Also to my parents for first giving me my love of wild places, the seas and mountains – a love that has stayed with me throughout my life.

Chapter 1

Meet the Family

I don't know exactly when my parents met, but I do know exactly where. I can give you the altitude (1788ft), National Grid reference (NY1915211425), longitude and latitude (54.49169°N, 3.24965°W) and I can even describe the view: the way that, to the east, the Ennerdale valley spread out behind them straight out of a geography textbook on glaciation and how to the south, sheltered by England's highest mountains, they could just see a glimpse of the top end of Wastwater. Wasdale Head, the hamlet on its eastern shore, likes to boast that it is the home of the highest mountain (Scafell Pike), the deepest lake (Wastwater), the smallest church (St Olaf's) and the biggest liar in England (a Victorian landlord at the Wasdale Head Hotel, when it was already on its way to being one of the most renowned climbers' hotels in the country). It must have meant a lot to them. They went back there every year they were married.

It's a peaceful spot, the Black Sail Pass – not a road but a bridlepath between Wasdale and Ennerdale in the western Lake District – and paradoxically it was even more peaceful in the middle of a world war. Because whatever the precise date that my parents met there, it was definitely sometime in the second half of 1943. My mother, Aline Eastwood, was 20 and training to be a teacher at a college in Ambleside, and was walking with a girlfriend over Black Sail Pass when they stopped to admire the view. My father, who was then 21 and on a walking holiday with a friend of his called Harry Parker, arrived just as they were still taking it all in. Would either of the girls, they wondered, be interested in sharing a bar of chocolate?

In 1943, you didn't have to ask that question twice. Chocolate was so heavily rationed that a small bar would have to last you a week. So the two women said yes, and got talking to the men. They mentioned that they'd spent the night in the youth hostel a couple of miles or so to the west. The two young men would have wanted to know more about it, because that's where they were going that night.

The Black Sail youth hostel (a former shepherd's bothy) was and is one of the most spectacularly situated in the whole of Britain. These days they've added a little extension on at the back so the warden no longer has to sleep in the common room, and it's been double-glazed, but remains inaccessible by road and is still relatively spartan. In 1943, it had only been open for ten years and was so basic that, for the first few years, it didn't bother with such luxuries as mattresses, opting instead for small dorms whose beds were made of canvas stretched over wooden poles. Women had to make do with a basin of water in their dormitory, men with the cold running water from the stream outside. There'd been some discussion about whether to bother keeping the Black Sail hostel open throughout the war, but in the end the association opted to keep it in use "as it was important to members from South Lancashire and West Yorkshire towns".

And that's what my Dad was. Like his friend Harry, he was an apprentice engineer working at Trafford Park in Manchester for Metro Vicks, as Metropolitan-Vickers was sometimes known. There was no question of either of them being called up to serve in the armed forces: Metro Vicks was one of the most important heavy engineering factories in the world and the work they were doing was just as valuable – if not more so – than anything they could have been doing at the front. It was Metro Vicks who made both the radar that helped win the Battle of Britain and the four-engined Lancaster heavy bombers which the previous year had started taking the fight to the enemy. In the course of the war, Lancasters would fly no fewer than 156,000 sorties. The firestorm raids on Hamburg in July that year and the Dambuster raids on the Ruhr dams in May were just two of them.

All his life, my father was passionate – to the point of obsession – about the need for Britain to train more and better engineers. That 21-year-old Metro Vicks apprentice became an internationally respected authority on the subject, and rose from leading research groups at the National Engineering Laboratory in East Kilbride to being the first professor in engineering at Salford University and setting up and chairing the Engineering Professors' Conference. In 1983, he was voted annual president of CIRP, the international academy for production engineering. There's only been one other Brit in that role from that day to this. Basically, if you were looking for one person in post-war Britain to spell out the importance of mechanical engineering, my father was that man.

Yet when I look back at my 21-year-old father walking with his mate up Black Sail Pass towards the woman who was to become his wife, I can understand why engineering mattered so much to him. As late as August 1943, apart from an Allied toehold on Sicily and the start of a Soviet pushback on the eastern front, every last country in Europe other than Britain was either under Axis rule or fearfully neutral. What could possibly turn the tide?

We didn't realise it at the time, but it was the productivity of the British wartime economy that was making a difference. Although after the war it was the efficiency of German engineering that won the world's admiration, during the war the British outshone them. In aircraft production alone, we were outpacing the Germans at a rate of two to one: by the end of the war, we had built 50,000 more planes. Alec's own brother-in-law John, who had moved from London to a job at the Necaco factory in Llanberis, north Wales, making wings for Wellington bombers, was himself also part of this same war on the engineering front – one that, in Britain, gave the Ministry of Aircraft Production priority over the manpower demands of the Army, Royal Navy and the RAF itself until as late as 1944. But it wasn't just a question of the numbers of workers: their productivity was important too. Earlier in 1943, another factory making Wellington bombers in north Wales – at Broughton, in Flintshire, smashed the American record for making a bomber from start to finish. The US record stood at a couple of days: the Welsh workers had their Wellington rolling out of the factory in a mere 24 hours.

Gradually, I notice, British military historians are starting to swing behind the thesis that the quality and innovation of British engineering was one of the key reasons that we won the Second World War. Without taking away from the heroism of my fathers' contemporaries who fought in British uniforms, the notion – based on Britain's post-war industrial decline – that this country just about muddled through the Second World War against a technologically superior enemy – a sort of Dad's Army fighting a nation of fascist super-engineers – is increasingly threadbare. Sadly, though, the new interpretation singling out the efficacy of British wartime engineering and productivity came too late for my Dad, who died in 2014. The first volume of James Holland's *The War in the West* was published the following year. I can imagine him reading it, and noting how much British technological innovation came out of places like Metro Vicks, how British engineering didn't just replace all of the materiel lost at Dunkirk for our own Army but provided a third of that used in Europe by the Americans too. "I told you British engineering mattered," I can just hear him saying, wagging a finger at me. "And you wouldn't have been free to be a doctor without it."

And just for once, I'll allow him the last laugh.

But let's get back to the Blacksail Pass, on that fateful day in 1943. When the two women had hiked off down one side of the pass, the two men strode off down the other. They arrived at the youth hostel less than an hour later. One of the first things they did was to look at the visitors' book. *Aline Mary Eastwood,* he read, and copied down the East Yorkshire address next to it. "I'll be writing to you," he thought to himself. And he did – which is why I'm here.

But there's another reason I like the story of how my parents first met. The view of what they would have known as Cumberland from the Black Sail Pass is of the wilder, remoter, western side of the Lake District. Even back then, the Keswick – Ambleside – Windermere central axis of the Lake District was increasingly filling up with charabancs and traffic. Few of them made it across the tortuous Hardknott and Wrynose passes to the altogether more peaceful western lakes. But at the Black Sail Pass, with its long gentle path down to Wastwater in one direction and Ennerdale Water on the other, those two young couples were miles from civilisation. The war which Alec and Harry were helping to win at Trafford Park could wait for another day; here they were as far away from it as they could get. At Black Sail hostel, one day apart, my father and mother could have watched the sun rise over Great Gable and set over Pillar Rock, the only Lake District summit that can't be reached without rock climbing. Indeed, many sources say that Lake District mountaineering began with the first ascent of Pillar Rock by a local man in 1825. Because mountaineering has been one of the grand passions of my own life, I'm rather glad of the small but not insignificant coincidence that right at the start of my story, before my life began, but somehow prefiguring it, there were mountains.

oooOOOooo

Approaching the end of my own life, I look back at the years my mother and father spent together before my birth and am amazed at the number of echoes I find. Just to the south of the Cuillin mountains on Skye, there is a loch to which I seem to have been drawn back like a salmon to the upper reaches of the river in which it was spawned. Loch Scavaig is a special place to me – so special that one day soon, a good friend will scatter my ashes on its waters. It's where I feel as though I belong.

In my mind, Loch Scavaig – and the jagged skyline of the mountains rearing majestically out of the sea – is associated with some of the very happiest times in my life. The Cuillin are part of it, of course, and I can think back to wonderful memories of climbing the Dubhs Ridge with my old climbing partner Gordon Taylor, or going back there almost every year in the last ten with Peter Davies, a good friend for almost all of my life, in *Liberty*, the yacht we share. Sailing is another passion in my life, just as mountaineering was before multiple sclerosis struck in my mid-twenties. Anchored on Loch Scavaig on a boat with friends, with the Cuillin in front of me,

I would have three of the great pleasures in life – friendship, mountains and the sea – all at hand.

Yet my mother and father got there first, and that dramatic corner of Scotland seems to have meant almost as much to them. When they got married on 29 March 1945, Harry Parker and Mary Skaife – the other couple formed at that meeting atop Black Sail Pass in 1943 – presented them with a wedding gift of great beauty. Personalised, detailed, funny and intricate, it is an illustrated record of a week-long climbing trip the four of them went on together to Skye over Easter 1944. Scrapbook is the wrong word, unless you think of the classiest scrapbook you've ever seen: here are routes they climbed on the Cuillins marked, along with the contours, in coloured pencils on tracing paper so precisely that you could follow them right now; cartoons of their mishaps and adventures, correspondence with their Glenbrittle landlady – a Mrs Chisholm as it happens (what are the odds?) – postcards, poems and photos and a week's diary all written up in flawless copperplate writing. It is the very best kind of wedding present: a labour of love.

I've got it in front of me as I write this, and as I turn the pages I again turn back to the war they were leaving behind. At Easter 1944, remember, Europe is still occupied, but the Allies are a third of the way up Italy and the Soviets are moving into the Crimea, eastern Poland and northern Romania. Lancasters are bombing targets in Germany and France almost every night: although the blackout is still enforced in Glasgow at night-time and Harry writes about the "chink of ice-axe against climbing boots" as they walk the quiet, darkened streets to drop off the two girls at the Church of Scotland hostel. All the same, there must have been a sense that the tide of war had changed. It still wasn't obvious to everybody, which is why the mountains were quieter than they'd been for years. "Climbers going to Skye were a somewhat unusual sight since the war" the wedding present scrapbook noted. For one thing, even to venture north of the Central Belt, they'd had to get a special military permit, and that kept the numbers down so much that they only encountered one other climber – a Canadian – on a generally sunny Easter week. "We thought with horror," my Dad noted, writing up a successful ascent of the Inaccessible Pinnacle via the White Slab route, "of the days of Peace when red and black funnelled steamers would hoot and wail to recall their flock of tourists back from [Loch] Coruisk to their hotels at Mallaig." We'll be revisiting Loch Coruisk later on: it's yet another one of those echoes across the decades, from their life to mine.

Of course, I'm biased, but they were impressive folks too, my parents. I've concentrated on my father so far, but what about my mother? How many other women climbed the Inaccessible Pinnacle that year? How many of them would think nothing of swimming in the sea – as both my parents did (in April, in Scotland: it must have been love) – or climbing through the snow and kicking out steps up No 3 Gully on Ben Nevis. When they did that, they looked up at Tower Ridge – another deep echo with a treasured memory from my own climbing days – and noted how impressive it looked: "It was almost black in contrast to the pure whiteness of the snow, which was dazzling with the sun shining on it."

These, then, were the two people who made me. When they got back to Glasgow with Harry and Mary Skaife, they went their separate ways once more. Mary caught the Edinburgh train from Queen Street Station, my mother caught the Hull train from St Enoch's (which is now a shopping mall). And Harry and Alec caught the train back to Manchester and their jobs as apprentice engineers at Metro Vicks. There was, after all, still a war on, and it wasn't won yet. I'll leave them to finish fighting it, and start with my own story.

Mountains, you will soon discover, have mattered a lot to me, but they mattered just as much to my parents. When they got married, they cut the wedding cake with an ice-axe.

oooOOOooo

Chapter 2

Made in Scotland

Officially at least, I belong to Glasgow. You wouldn't have been able to tell that from my accent for the last 50 years, and I haven't worn a kilt in Chisholm tartan in ages, but "born in Glasgow" is indeed what it says on my passport and birth certificate, even if I am one of that rare breed of Glaswegians who don't particularly mind if England beat Scotland at football, rugby or indeed anything else. For it was in a Glasgow maternity hospital that my lungs first breathed in air on 21 October 1951, and the Chisholms' first family home to which they brought me back was a three-bedroomed pebble-dashed semi on Lindsay Road, East Kilbride.

It's hard to imagine now, but back then East Kilbride – eight miles south-east of Glasgow – was one of the most forward-looking places in Britain. In 1947, it became the first "new town" in Scotland, and the following year the Mechanical Engineering Research Laboratory was built there. Although it soon changed its name to the National Engineering Laboratory, it didn't change its purpose – to be at the cutting edge of British engineering research and development, with a budget overshadowed only by those for similar establishments in the US and the USSR. It was here, my father hoped, where Britain's second industrial revolution would be forged, where research scientists like him would open up our future as a science superpower. Armed with a hard-won first-class degree in engineering that he had taken at the Royal Technical College, Salford while working as an apprentice at Metro Vicks, he moved north to what looked distinctly like the job of his dreams.

At the National Engineering Laboratory, if nowhere else, he found somewhere that implemented his belief that Britain should honour its engineering heritage and build on it in the future. Each of the NEL's huge research laboratories was named after a British pioneer in the field to which it was devoted. Henry Maudslay, Joseph Bramah, William Rankine, Joseph Whitworth: why weren't they every bit as famous, my father would have wondered, as, say, Trollope, Wordsworth, Dickens and Austen? I can certainly imagine him making the case. "Look Roger," I can hear him saying, "they've changed our lives so much more. Machine tools, the hydraulic press, thermodynamics, mass production: each one of those four men has revolutionised industry – and yet the way we ignore engineering, you'd be lucky to meet anyone who's ever heard of them."

I am, you've probably gathered, leaping ahead of myself, because my Dad almost certainly wasn't saying this to his swaddled newborn son held in his wife's arms in the back seat as he drove from the maternity hospital to our East Kilbride home. It was only in my teens when he started putting pressure on me to study engineering at university.

Apart from the job, there were other important reasons my parents had looked forward to coming to Scotland. I've already mentioned their love of climbing and walking, but my father also adored sailing. He may have failed to pass on his passion for engineering to me, but there's one transference that *did* work: I've always been happiest messing around on boats. Indeed, it's been the one consistent golden thread in my life. Whatever else has disappointed me in life, that love of being on a boat surging through water with the bow wave singing, never has.

Where did that start? In our family album, there's a photo of me standing on the bow of a yacht, holding onto the shrouds (the wire ropes holding up the mast), and looking straight ahead, my three-year-old head with its back to the camera. It's 1954, we're on the Clyde, a slight breeze is coming over the beam and gently filling the heavy tan-coloured canvas sails. If I were Proust, I'd be able to give you five pages about that boy and that moment, the way it now seems so timeless and dreamlike, a colour shot from a usually monochrome decade. It might be something to do with the fact that you can't see my face, but you can see where we're heading. There's a gentle wind, a calm sea, clouds clearing or gathering (clearing, I think) in the distance at the head of the loch. This boy, I think, as I look at the picture, knows that he's found something he's always going to love: holding onto a rope, and starting out on an adventure.

Is that too much hindsight? Of course it is. But look at what I can't remember about the first seven years of my life – the Scotland years – and what I can. I can remember wearing a kilt (Chisholm tartan, naturally) to Jackton primary school in East Kilbride but not too much more about it. I can remember my sister Diana making an appearance as a baby in our Lindsay Road home when I was three, but hardly anything else about what it looked like inside. Yet when I think back to the facts about those seven years that I *can* drag back from the murk of oblivion, they all seem to have one thing in common. See if you can identify what. First, that my Dad was one of the founder-members of the NEL Sailing Club in 1952 and its first commodore. Second, that one of his best friends went on to be Commodore at St Mawes Sailing Club in Cornwall. And – last but not least – the names of the two GP 14 dinghies built by the East Kilbride engineers for their sailing club[1] were Tamarisk, which was painted red, and the Scilla, which was blue. It's odd, isn't it, the things that stick in a seven-year-old boy's mind? Odd too, isn't it, that they're all about sailing?

But if I'm technically Scottish, I'm English and Welsh too. English because both my parents were, and because that's where I've lived and worked for six decades. And Welsh because back in 1940, part of my extended family moved there and my Mum and Dad partially followed them. I'd better introduce you to my father's side of the family. In 1940, his father (also Alec), a former architect who had been gassed in the First World War, was living in Chester, where he'd just moved from Liverpool with his wife Maude. They had five

---

1 Many of this group remained lifelong friends. Recently, when taking a boat through the Crinan Canal, it was pointed out that the average age of the crew was well over 80!

grown-up children: four sisters – Margaret, Katherine, Jean, Dorothea – and my father, who was then 18. I'll concentrate for now on Katherine, because of all the four sisters, she was the one whose own life indirectly had the greatest effect on my own.

Katherine and her husband John had moved to Chester from London, where he had worked in a furrier's, having been trained as a fur salesman in Harrod's. But when he was called up for war work at a factory in Llanberis making wings for Wellington bombers, off they went by train to Caernarfon and started looking for a place to live.

And that, in 1940, was a lot harder than you might have thought. Snowdonia was crowded out with Londoners fleeing the Blitz. At the village of Brynrefail, at the western end of a lake called Llyn Padarn, a Mrs Thomas let Kath and John stay in her front bedroom. The next day, after John had cycled off to start his new job, Kath and Mrs Thomas walked along the shore of Llyn Padarn. In years to come, I would get to know that lake very well indeed. So well, in fact, that not too far away is the second and last place I'd like my ashes to be scattered.

But back to 1940. As Kath and Mrs Thomas walked east from Brynrefail they took a narrow, winding road along the lake towards a hamlet called Fachwen. "I thought it was like paradise," Kath wrote years later, "the pine trees on the left, among huge chunks of pre-Cambrian rock, and on the right, over a wall, there was a lake, reflecting Snowdon."

At Fachwen, they found a primitive cottage – no electricity, no running water, but theirs for 2/6d a week. For that, they got a wood at the back with owls and woodpeckers, nights lit up with glow-worms and days lit up by that fantastic view south across the lake where she had first seen Snowdon's reflection. Although she didn't know it at the time, about a mile away on the other side of the lake, that view also included a cottage that would, for a full half century, be my "home from home".

So that's the Welsh bit of me. A cottage half-way up a mountain-side, with views not only back towards Fachwen – where my cousin Richard lives to this day – but to the mountains of Snowdonia beyond. Those mountains are where another part of me began. I can't remember when and where my father first handed me a climbing rope, but Snowdon was just seven miles away from our cottage at Clegir, and it is on its rocky sides that I first learnt the basics of mountaineering – just as it was there – on Clogwyn y Person – that I made my final climb.

I always think of Snowdon as Britain's most democratic mountain. Thanks to its mountain railway, it is Britain's busiest one: its summit often packed with ice-cream eating tourists and day-trippers who, on a good day, can see not just Wales but Ireland, Scotland and England. Yet it is also a mountain with its own secrets and challenges, which is why Edmund Hillary used to train there for his Everest expedition, and why a handful of years earlier, as the Second World War wound down to a close and their married life began, my parents would climb there too.

Before they bought their Clegir cottage nearly two decades later, Alec and Aline would stay at Fachwen on their climbing weekends away from Manchester. And although Kathleen and John moved away to Shropshire in 1952, they liked the view across Llyn Padarn so much that they soon started renting a different three-bedroomed quarryman's cottage in Fachwen, which they finally bought in the mid-1960s. In the meanwhile, they had two children – first of all my cousin Richard, born in 1943, and so eight years older than me, and then – just 17 months later, cousin Rosemary.

What this all meant was that, for some of my childhood summers at least, Richard and Rosemary would be staying on one side of the lake with their parents and Diana and I would be staying with ours on the other. Every childhood should have its halcyon moments, and these were mine, paddling away on my cousins' canoes on Llyn Padarn in what – yes, I know it's a cliché, and maybe memory does indeed blot out the clouds – seem to have been endlessly sunny summers. My parents had an old two-seater canoe which was much heavier, but I always preferred the single-seaters – or taking out the small cadet sailing dinghy which cousin Richard had built for himself. Maybe it wasn't quite *Swallows and Amazons* (Richard and Rosemary were just those few, but significant, years older than the

two of us for it to be like that), but they were endless days of freedom and adventure nonetheless.

That's how it seemed to me anyway, but Richard and Rosemary
remember it differently. "Our parents used to let us play and do our
own thing," she told me when I checked to see that our memories
tallied. "Your mother and father pushed you endlessly. Education
was the be-all and end-all. I remember Mum saying, 'I think Roger's
parents are pushing him a bit too much – you know, like having to
do homework, even in the holidays.'" "Your father could be quite
forceful," Richard added. "I never saw him lose his temper but he
certainly pushed you both very hard."

They're right: education did matter to my father, largely because
he'd had to struggle to get one. In 1934, his father had sent him off
from the family home in Broad Green, Liverpool, to Brentwood
School in Essex aged 12 but he had to pull him out a couple of years
later because he couldn't afford the £240 a year fees. (The family
finances had crashed so disastrously in the mid-Thirties that they had
to hide their furniture from the bailiffs). Leaving school without qual-
ifications, my father was barely into his teens when he was searching
out jobs for himself in London. The first one he found was working
at an engineering office at Waterloo Station at 10/- a week, then he
moved on to work for the Admiralty as a lab assistant at Teddington,
before heading back north to work as an apprentice engineer at Metro
Vicks in Manchester. That's where he was working when this story
began, in 1943, with him meeting my mother on Black Sail Pass.

Look, though, at what he'd done since. He'd worked his way up
from being a Metro Vicks apprentice to graduating with a first in
engineering (an external London University degree he took while at
the Royal Technical College, Salford). He'd worked, as we've seen,
as a research scientist at the National Engineering Laboratory in
East Kilbride. So starry was his research there that it propelled him
to Washington DC for an 18-month stint as a scientific attaché. In
1957, he came back to Salford, this time as head of mechanical engineering at the Royal Technical College. In the next decade, it
became, first of all a college of advanced technology and finally, in
1967, a university. When that happened, he became its first

professor of mechanical engineering, and his department, with 64 full-time staff, was the second-biggest of its kind in the country.

So yes: a driven man. And as for education being "the be-all and end-all", well, perhaps when you're on course to being a professor and you marry a teacher it does indeed shoot up the list of priorities you want for your children. There was always, though, more to them than that. I've only got to go into the front room of my house to remind myself of how much more.

On each side of the fireplace, there are five shelves crammed with books about mountaineering and sailing. Most of them are mine, but plenty of them came down to me from my parents. Here's one: *Mountaineering in Scotland* by WH Murray, that great classic of mountaineering literature published in 1947 and written originally on toilet paper in a prisoner of war camp: the Gestapo found it and destroyed the book, but Murray just began it all again. (Maybe, I think to myself with a smile, in Easter 1944 my Mum and Dad were climbing the very peaks that Murray was dreaming of in captivity.) "It seems such a little while since I first enjoyed this book" my father wrote on the frontispiece of a copy he bought for me two decades later, and there are plenty more: about expeditions to Annapurna, early attempts on Everest, or the more spectacular adventures of Bill Tillman.

Those TE Lawrences and Thesigers on the shelves came, among many more, from my mother. They were dreamers, those two, even if they slotted into suburbia with a predictable dream of raising their children to get their lives off to a flying start by being good at exams, they still wanted to read – as I always have myself – about lives lived on the cusp of danger, of pumping adrenalin and desperate odds against survival. My father was the more practical of the two; my mother – as you might perhaps expect from an art teacher (though she also taught PE) the dreamier. Once, according to family folklore, she bought a decrepit boat on a beach in Filey for £5. "Someday," she insisted, "we'll sail round the world in that." Well, we never did, and I occasionally wonder what happened to that £5 boat of her dreams. By now, I suspect, it will have long ago rotted away into the Filey sands.

But back, for the moment, to suburbia, this time not to my own front room but to the first house my father bought after we moved back down to England from Scotland. The first, and as it happens, the last, because although he moved into 12 Legh Road, Prestbury, along with his wife and young family in 1958, he only left it when he died in 2014.

These days, Prestbury – "one of Britain's poshest villages" according to the *Daily Mail* – only skims briefly into the public consciousness when a famous footballer like Wayne Rooney decides to buy a house there. Part of Cheshire's "Golden Triangle" along with Wilmslow and Alderley Edge, the village just outside Macclesfield is now one of the more expensive places to live outside London. We got there long before the footballers moved in, because it was a handy commute for my Dad from the nearby station to Salford and was just two and a half miles away from Tytherington School in Macclesfield, where my Mum taught.

Again, let's have some context. When they moved, in 1958, that school had just been open a year. All the houses on Legh Road were new too, their gardens bare of flowers and bushes. In a small way, both of these were part of that newer Britain that was finally emerging after all the blood, sweat, tears and finally cleared bombsites of the Second World War. This was the Britain that was, in the Sixties, introducing the E-Type Jaguar (1961), cross-channel hovercraft (1968) and helping to get Concorde ready for its test flight (1969). All, you'll notice, something to do with mechanical engineering – the very subject about which Dad was trying to instil in me, an enthusiasm that matched his own by getting me to help take apart and rebuild the engine in our Vauxhall Victor. I was 15 at the time, and my future was unclouded and clear. I was going to be, like him, an engineer. An engineer who would spend all of his free time sailing and climbing, but an engineer nonetheless.

That young would-be engineer had been, from 1963, a pupil at Brentwood School in Essex. I'd got in at all the schools I applied for – Manchester Grammar, Cheadle Hulme, and Abingdon were also on the list – but my father was adamant that I go to Brentwood. Maybe it was unfinished business: this time there would be a

Chisholm who would head south and stay the whole course, not be forced to quit when the family's money ran out. Secretly, I was rather glad to get away from him. My father could be very intense and hard-driving: if I'd remained at home, he would probably have had rows with me about not studying hard enough. "Look Roger," I can hear him say, "you should be concentrating on your studies not spending all your time fencing."

Fencing? He'd have been right about that. I was never any good at ball sports, but Brentwood had a great record at fencing, and indeed I was captain of the fencing team in the year in which we won the public schools championships. I was a sabreur – the kind of fencing in which you can score by using the side of the (very blunt) blade as well as its point – and a good one too: I can still remember all the parrying and blocking positions, even though it's years since my body was able to follow my brain and put them into practice.

The non-fencing part of my brain was working well too. In 1969, I got As in Mathematics, Further Mathematics and Physics and the top grade in S-level Physics. Apart from those people seriously interested in going to Oxbridge, hardly anyone bothered with S-levels. But I was interested, passed my Cambridge entrance exam, and in 1970, I went up to St John's to read engineering. Before I did, I had already won a Rolls-Royce Scholarship that meant my university years wouldn't cost me a penny.

One of the conditions of the scholarship was that from January to August 1970 I had to work at Rolls-Royce's Derby factory, where it makes its aero engines. Like my father at Metro Vicks all those years ago, I was an apprentice engineer. I was even a project manager. There were about 20 of us – all undergraduates, and though I was the only one on a full scholarship paid for by Rolls-Royce, others had bursaries. Different groups were allocated different tasks. Ours was to make a photocopying illuminator from scratch. We had to build a machine that gave constant light across a clearly defined area, using a camera that had to be immensely adjustable and capable of moving across six feet, complete with illumination, mirrors, controls – and all the working parts had to be made using milling machines, lathes and turning machines, right down to the last hand-made screw. At the end of the three-month project, the group I led won first prize. Subsequent months were spent attached to a variety of departments, shadowing working engineers.

The best A- and S-level results possible. The only Rolls-Royce industrial scholarship. A place at Cambridge to read engineering. In September 1970, as I left Prestbury to go up to Cambridge, my father couldn't have been more pleased with me. Like father, like son: the Chisholms would be engineers who made the world sit up and pay attention.

Then it all started to go downhill.

oooOOOooo

Chapter 3

Charlie 54

Where does the story of me and mountains really begin? With my father throwing down a rope in some long-lost childhood summer afternoon when I was ten or 11, watching as I tied it in a knot around my waist and guiding me up on a boulder below our North Wales cottage? Those times he took me along to try out some of the easier routes on Laddow Rocks, the gritstone outcrop in the Peak District where he and his best friend Harry used to test themselves on harder climbs? What moment did climbing become something that I *had* to do rather than just rather liked doing?

All I can say is that by the time I was 18, I had started to fall under its spell. I would never be an extreme climber, I would never push myself to foolish risks, I didn't really like soloing, and yes, you could even say that I was cautious. But I understood the joys of climbing just as much as anyone. The way it involved all the senses at once. The way touch suddenly became almost as important as sight – the feel of rock beneath your fingers, working out the hardness or slipperiness of the hold, your fingers exploring all the indentations on the rock, your boots testing out the little ledge you are standing on – just a little bit of pressure, but not committing to it unless you were absolutely sure. At times, when all of your senses were fully engaged, sharpened by a frisson of risk, climbing gave me something of the same feeling that sailing has always done. Sailing and climbing were the great passions in my life, just as they had been for my parents, and I could never choose between them.

Certainly, by the summer of 1970, when I was working as an apprentice engineer for Rolls-Royce, that love of climbing had intensified. After the working week in the factory in Derby – first of all on that prize-winning made-from-scratch photocopying illuminator project, then on a series of secondments to various departments – I would positively yearn for the weekend, for the trips to Snowdonia with my fellow apprentices, when I would once again discover that joy in the body's fluidity, of being in control, of moving safely amid danger, that climbing gives. At the same time, though, it imposes its own stillness and moments of concentration, like when you work out the line you'll take across the rock, or pause while your nose brushes lichen or your suddenly-appearing face sends a beetle scurrying away into a tiny crevice you might want to use as a handhold. At times like that, while I couldn't be freer, I also felt as though I couldn't be any closer to the world.

I was working as a Rolls-Royce apprentice in the nine months between finishing school and going to Cambridge when I attempted my first ever "real climb", on the vertically splintered volcanic rock slabs of Cwm Idwal in Snowdonia. It's called the Ordinary Route, though there wasn't very much that was ordinary about the apprentice, also 18, with whom I went up it – Henry Hornyold-Strickland, eldest son of the 7th Count della Cantena and soon to be the eighth himself. Henry grew up in Sizergh Castle, near Kendal, where the Stricklands had lived for 750 years (one ancestor carried the flag of St George at Agincourt). He was about to go to Oxford to read engineering, I was about to do the same at Cambridge. I lost touch with Count Henry pretty much straight away, but there's one thing we will always have in common. It was his first proper climb too.

We went back to Cwm Idwal on other weekends and polished off separate climbs there called Faith, Hope and Charity (all good routes for learning multi-pitching). Gradually I was tackling harder and harder routes and really starting to take my climbing seriously. By the time I went to Cambridge in September 1970, there was one club out of the 300-plus looking for new members in Fresher's Week that I couldn't wait to join.

I already knew a bit about the Cambridge University Mountaineering Club (CUMC) because my mother had previously bought me a copy of its journal at Joe Brown's climbing gear shop in Llanberis. I've probably still got it somewhere. I'd actually heard of some of the people who were writing in it, I'd read about their exploits. I knew that the club, founded in 1906, was one of the oldest of its kind in Britain, that its past members were legendary, their climbs the kind of adventures I have always found inspiring. Non-climbers might scoff at the very notion of a mountaineering club slap bang in the middle of what is almost the flattest part of England, but I knew better.

At Fresher's Week, they told me how to join. In 1970, the club's president, Oliver Overstall, was in my college, with rooms three floors up in North Court. I can still remember standing outside his door, feeling slightly nervous. There was music playing inside. I gave a tentative knock.

It must have been evening. I remember that the lighting was subdued, and that inside the room there were two men, both sitting on beanbags, listening to Melanie. If you're not as old as me, you're going to be asking "Melanie who?" And I'm going to have to reach far back into the annals of rock history, back to Woodstock the previous year, where Melanie, a doe-eyed 1960s flower-child with an ethereal voice, took to the stage on the first night of festival in front of an audience of 400,000 people getting drenched in the pouring rain. At the end of her half-hour set (the Incredible String Band had refused to play in the rain) she was singing *Beautiful People* when she looked up and saw a sea of lit cigarette lighters in raised hands. Later, that memory inspired her to write *Lay Down (Candles in the Rain)*, and it was on the B-side of the record that was playing as I entered the room.

I introduced myself to Overstall, and he introduced me to another 18-year-old from the north-west of England – in this case, Wallasey. "Alan Rouse. Maybe you've heard of him?"

Of course I'd heard of Alan Rouse. Everyone had. He was British climbing's teenage prodigy. Earlier that summer, he'd had soloed The Boldest on Clogwyn Du'r Arddu, or "Cloggy" as it is invariably known to climbers – the north flank of Snowdon and, in British climbing circles widely considered just about the best climbing cliff in the country. There are scores of routes up it, ranging from, in ascending order, difficult (D), hard difficult (HD), very difficult (VD), hard very difficult (HVD), severe (S), hard severe (HS), hard very severe (HVS) and extremely severe (E). Once you get into the E category, it starts splitting up again: E1, E2, E3 and so on. The Boldest is ranked at E4 for overall difficulty, and has a similarly high mark (5c) for technical difficulty. So when I met the 18-year-old Alan Rouse, who had ostensibly come to Cambridge to read mathematics at Emmanuel – I say ostensibly, because half of the time he should have been studying he was usually halfway up some Scottish or Welsh crag instead – I already knew that he was a climber in a different league to me. After all, here was a man who, that year, had climbed an E4 5c, a route that was at the time regarded as one of the hardest climbs in the country. By himself, and without ropes.

Sixteen years later, Alan Rouse became the first Briton to climb K2, the world's second highest mountain and deadliest peak. Stuck in a snowstorm on the way down, he died.

I can't say that we were close. In many ways, we were opposites. With his long, tousled hair and aviator glasses, he looked like a Scouse version of Peter Fonda in *Easy Rider*, the hit film of the previous year. Certainly Rouse was looking for adventure or whatever came his way: in a book his friend Geoff Birtles put together shortly after his death, Rouse admitted that he was a "womaniser" who "liked to live on the edge".[2]

Certainly, he was an extrovert; definitely, he was sociable and liked a drink. I was neither: well, I wasn't teetotal, and I wasn't anti-social, and at Cambridge I would certainly pop into The Baron of Beef or The Pickerel for the occasional pint with friends. Rouse, however, was reckless in a way I never was and firmly part of what climber-writer John Porter called "a generation that nearly climbed itself into extinction".[3] He was a brilliant climber, but he always risked a lot more than I could ever imagine. In 1972, for example, when I edited the *CUMC Journal*, it is somehow only typical that his

2 Birtles, Geoff, *Alan Rouse: A Mountaineer's Life*, HarperCollins, 1987
3 Porter, John: *One Day as a Tiger*, Vertebrate, 2015

contribution to it was a bravura piece written with dazzling sang-froid about a near-disaster while attempting the south face of the Aiguille du Fou above Chamonix when a piton came out of the rock and he fell 15 feet. "My foot seemed to be growing out of my leg at a rather peculiar angle and a quick prod revealed a certain amount of pain, so putting two and two together I decided my ankle was broken". It took him 17 one-legged abseils to get to the bottom of the couloir and rescue.

My own climbing career never touched those heights, or those dramas, or those fears. Just as, when sailing, I only ever sailed in a gale once in my life (and that wasn't my fault: I was 17 and crewing), in all my time on the mountains, I never once fell. That's relatively unusual, and climbers of a higher standard than I ever reached quite often fell onto their ropes – or sometimes, as with legendary climbers like Joe Brown – fell the height of a house without them. But I never once fell off through loss of control. And I'm proud of that.

Meanwhile, term had started and like every other first-year student at Cambridge, I spent the first few weeks getting used to the place and feigning nonchalance living for three years in such a stunningly beautiful place (King's College Chapel, the Backs etc.). Back then, of course, all the colleges were still single-sex, and the university was run according to a welter of rules and traditions. Some of these are still maintained to this day, such as that academic gowns have to be worn for meals in hall and that cleaners are called "bedders". Many, however, have fallen by the wayside such as that the university was policed by its own constables, called bulldogs, who patrolled the colleges wearing top hats and wielding furled umbrellas. They were on the lookout for major misdemeanours such as male students trying to smuggle women into their rooms after the college shut its gates for the night, or slightly inebriated members of the CUMC going night-climbing after their annual dinner.

As an engineering student, I would sometimes envy those studying for arts degrees whose working week might only consist of a single one-on-one tutorial and however little time it took them to write an essay for it. We had it a lot tougher. Six days a week, I'd cycle down the Trumpington Road to the engineering laboratories, where teaching or lab work started at 9am and finished at 1pm, usually with a whole load of practical problem papers to stuff into my briefcase and spend most of the rest of the day puzzling over.

Still, there were some compensations. After Brentwood, I knew I was good at fencing, but I wanted to widen that out to include other sports. Modern pentathlon seemed a good bet – swimming, shooting, show jumping and cross-country too – so I joined the Modern Pentathlon Club. In my second year, I was its treasurer and won a Half Blue after being selected as one of the six-strong team which represented Cambridge (unsuccessfully, alas) in the annual match against Oxford.

I also learnt to fly. In my first year, I applied to join the University Air Squadron, which at the time meant – it's hard to imagine it happening now – 18-year-old students being trained for free by qualified RAF instructors. Because of that, selection was incredibly competitive, yet when I got picked I realised that I'd have to turn down the place because I'd just got too much on, what with my holiday commitments to Rolls-Royce, the promise to join my parents on the family holiday, and all the climbs with friends I'd lovingly been pencilling into the diary. I don't know for sure, but I got the distinct impression that nobody had ever turned them down before. In my second year, I promised, it would be different. I thought they would wash their hands of me, but to my surprise they kept me on their books. If I wanted to, they agreed, they would teach me – not just how to fly solo but how to do aerobatics too.

All of which made my Cambridge second year a bit of an *annus mirabilis*. Looking back now – even looking back just five years later – it seems hard to imagine that I could do everything I was doing then. Cycling down the Newmarket Road for 20 minutes, breezing into the flight room at Marshall's Airfield, opening the locker and getting out my flying kit, picking up my parachute, checking that I had clearance to fly and then walking out across the grass airstrip where my plane was waiting for me.

De Havilland had stopped making the Chipmunk back in 1956, but they were such serviceable aircraft – and so easy to fly, which is why they made such great trainer aircraft – and many are still airworthy today. By the time I was being taught how to fly, most air forces had replaced them with jet trainers such as the BAC Jet Provost. The Chipmunk, in fact, was such an old plane that when it first came into service in 1946, it was usually as a replacement for the Tiger Moth biplane – a fact which really does make me feel old!

But the Chipmunk was a lovely little plane all the same. In my mind's eye, I can still see it waiting for me on the airstrip, yellow chocks wedged against the wheels underneath the wings, silver-grey fuselage glinting in the sun, the long double cockpit, with room for the trainer behind the novice pilot, vivid red flashes on the front facings of the wings and on either side of the engine, with RAF roundels and tail-fin markings and the University Air Squadron's insignia on the fuselage next to the wing.

The Chipmunk was too boxy to be beautiful, nothing remotely like the Spitfire. Except in one thing, which films about the Second World War never really show because none of them seem to have been shot from the pilot's point of view while taxiing prior to take-off. Once airborne, when the plane flies horizontally, you wouldn't notice it; but when the plane is taxiing towards take-off you certainly do. Because the plane "sits up" on its front two wheels, when you are the pilot and looking straight ahead, nearly all you can see in front of you is the plane's nose, and the blur of the propeller. So, as you get ready for take-off, just in order to see straight ahead, you have to weave slightly from side to side.

My call sign was Charlie 54, and once the control tower had given me clearance to take off, that's exactly what I would have been doing, moving the Chipmunk slightly from side to side as the engine roared and we sped across the runway grass. Then up, up, and away over Ely, maybe to the aerobatic area over the East Anglian Fens. The wonder of it all was how little time it took to learn to fly, how little time it was – maybe just eight hours – before you were allowed to go solo. The instructor would come back and show you how to do a particular manoeuvre – a loop, say – but the next time you'd be doing it by yourself. Looping the loop was the first piece of aerobatics that you'd learn, but soon there'd be so much more. Barrel rolls, stall turns, spins, dives: we were never going to be the Red Arrows, but up in the Cambridgeshire sky, we at least got a hint of what it felt like to push a flying machine further than you might have thought either it – or you – could go.

At the end of my second year, the squadron held a two-week summer camp at RAF Scampton in Lincolnshire – which, ironically, is where the Red Arrows are based these days although they weren't back then. Instead, they had something even more spectacular – the massive delta-winged Vulcan bombers which were technically still able to carry nuclear weapons even though for the last three years the main British deterrent were the Polaris submarines which first went on patrol from Faslane in 1968. The Vulcans certainly looked deterring, and my Dad would have probably seen in them yet another example of British engineering at its best. Massive, sleek and menacing, the Vulcans fit perfectly into iconography of Cold War Armageddon. Those four Bristol Siddeley Olympus engines I'd seen being made at Rolls-Royce in Derby might, for the moment, be powering a Vulcan flying over the turnip fields of Lincolnshire. But it didn't take too much to imagine the Vulcan squadron of 617 Squadron – the successor to the famous Dambusters – roaring off, carrying a Blue Danube, a Violet Club, a Yellow Sun, or a Red Beard or any of the other colourfully named nuclear bombs that would extinguish life on a scale few could properly imagine. When those engines were running at about 90 per cent, some quirk of design in the air vents meant that they emitted the most enormous howl or, occasionally, a truly scary whistle. I've never seen a more awesome plane. That summer camp at Scampton, sometimes I'd be doing circuits in my little Chipmunk and I'd look across at the Vulcans, flying at roughly the same height, doing pretty much the same thing. Five professional warriors in one; in the other, a student who was beginning to have doubts about engineering as a career but who still hadn't decided what to do with his life.

Not all my discoveries at Cambridge were quite so loud or dramatic. In fact, one of the biggest could hardly have been quieter – or closer. The Wherry Library is one of the smaller libraries in

Cambridge – when I was there it probably had approximately 1,000 books and journals – and in my first year at St John's they were all kept at the top of a tower in Chapel Court, off which I had my own rooms in my first year.

Appropriately enough for a collection of books about climbing, the library housing them was at the top of a winding wooden spiral staircase that itself began three floors up. Yet in that tower room, a young climber could find everything to whet his interest. Books about the great climbers who first ventured into the Himalaya in the 19th century. About the pioneers – so many of them British – who came up with the strange idea that mountains – in the Alps, in the Lake District, in Scotland, anywhere on Earth – were there to be climbed, and that doing so was enjoyable as well as dangerous. Moreover, because the CUMC had reciprocal links with similar clubs all over the world, there were journals from Canada, Australia, America too – all spreading the gospel of adventure that had first intrigued me in the pages of the mountaineering books on the shelves of our home in Prestbury.

Sometimes you'll hear people say that there are no great adventures to be had in the world any more, now that all the highest mountains have been conquered and all the main rivers explored. I can understand why people think that, because I can't deny that in those quiet hours in the Wherry Library, the books that held the greatest appeal were by those very climbers and explorers who had done so much to open up the planet. There they were on the library shelves, book after book of memoirs by those globe-striding late Victorians, with lithograph prints on crinkly paper, and barely plausible, Shackleton-like levels of derring-do in the stories within.

Even on the relatively easy slabs of Cwm Idwal earlier that summer, I'd caught a glimpse of why climbing mattered. And in the pages of those mountaineering journals, there was always a section on "new routes". The mountain might have been conquered, but there were always new ways of reaching the top. And even when you were retracing a climb so commonplace that the rocks themselves were polished by the boots of those who had climbed it for the last century or so, well, you were still part of that communion of climbers who were not just moving slowly up Earth's higher, or more secret and inaccessible places, but were also moving higher in their own ability to master increasingly difficult routes.

Those "new routes" were opening up everywhere. In my second year at university, when I edited the *CUMC Journal*, our own club alone accounted for 17 of them. Eight were notched up by a few of the club's graduating third-years who, wanting to go beyond the usual Alpine routes, had headed off to Arctic Norway in an old butcher's van to have a crack at unclimbed granite peaks south of Narvik. Mick Geddes, a lanky Scot studying chemical engineering at Pembroke College, who as club president invited me to a fateful Ben Nevis meet in April 1972, had been particularly busy the previous year, making first ascents of no fewer than five Scottish routes as well as the first winter ascent of Orion North Face Direct on Ben Nevis for more than a decade. I liked Geddes. He was the other teenage climbing prodigy in the university in my year. Just days before he started at Cambridge – on 13 September, 1970, when he was still 18 – he had become the youngest person ever to climb all the Munros (the 282 peaks higher than 3,000ft in Scotland).

I was nowhere near as classy a climber as Geddes, but I was determined to improve, to push myself harder. At the end of 1970's Michaelmas term – in other words, at the start of the Christmas holidays – I got my first chance.

I'd already volunteered to be the librarian looking after the Wherry collection, but now I wanted to start measuring myself against the achievement of the climbers I had read about. I'd met a fellow-engineer called Gordon Taylor, from Selwyn College, through the CUMC and we teamed up together on a ten-day club meet on the granite sea cliffs at Bosigran, on the north Cornish coast six miles west of St Ives. Every day on our stay, the sun shone. And every day Gordon and I could make our way back to the Count House climbing hut near an abandoned tin mine with a degree more confidence. As the Atlantic rolled in beneath us, the standard of our climbing was slowly getting better, to the point at which climbs graded VS (Very Severe) no longer seemed impossibly intimidating.

Ten days, and my climbing year wasn't finished yet. On the last day of 1970, Gordon came to stay at the cottage. Just to prove that VS routes no longer had any fear for us, we went up Sabre Cut – a 55-metre climb often thought to be the best VS route in Llanberis Pass – even though it was dusted with a light powdery snow. And even when we got back to the cottage, we still weren't finished climbing for the day.

I'd met Carl and Dennis, a couple of Catholic priests in training, at Borrowdale Youth Hostel earlier that year. There had been snow on the tops, and I tagged along with them up Great Gable and a few other summits. I was glad of their company, because back then I had still got a lot to learn about climbing and I'm not 100 per cent sure that I would have been completely safe even just scrambling on the tops in such conditions. As I said earlier, I'm a cautious climber, and I know my limits.

Anyway, I invited them to the cottage for New Year, and along with Gordon we walked down to the Padarn Hotel, which in those days was a place where you could expect to meet a lot of other climbers. We had a couple of pints and headed off up to Snowdon. It was a perfect winter night, the mountains covered with snow, and a bright moon in a cold, clear night sky. The Snowdon Mountain Railway starts yards away from the Padarn, and for much of the way we followed its tracks, because the snow was banked quite high elsewhere. We left the hotel at about nine o'clock and we made it up to the top of Snowdon with about half an hour to spare. Looking back, we could see the head-torches of a few people who'd had the same idea as us but were still struggling up the mountain, zig-zagging up the Pyg route and possibly stuck on an icy stretch.

Strictly speaking, the eighth decade of the 20th century began that night at a second after midnight. The four of us – two trainee priests and two engineering students – on the snow-covered summit of Wales's highest mountain, celebrated with small tots of whisky from a bottle Gordon had brought. We had some Christmas cake too.

I look back affectionately on the four of us at the start of that new decade. Later on, for me at least, it would bring two different kinds of heartbreak, two different kinds of the world crumbling away beneath my feet. For now, though, the moon shone down on the snowy summits, whisky warmed us, and life was just about as good as it could possibly be.

oooOOOooo

Chapter 4

Tower Ridge

There is a corner of Scotland that is particularly precious to me. To be fair, lots of corners of Scotland are precious to me, especially on the west coast. But there's one corner that I seem to be drawn to more than most. It's where the Black Cuillin soar from the sea like angry gods, their jagged peaks threatening and imposing even from a distance. Maybe with me it's the fact that they rise *from the sea* that counts, because that's how I first saw them, as we nosed north, past Rum and Canna, on *Zuleika*, a yacht Dad chartered for our family holiday in 1969. And there they were in front of us, growing larger and more menacing with each passing mile as we neared Loch Scavaig: Sgurr Alasdair and his attendant gang of gabbro peaks – all, at a mere 55 million years old, the youngest in the country, the sharpest pointed, the least weathered, least tamed, the most raw.

Tourists have been coming to this most geologically dramatic corner of Scotland for years. Loch Coruisk, the small but perfectly formed freshwater loch separated from the sea by the short River Scavaig and a vast slab of glaciated rock – is the secret heart of these mountains: shaded, roadless, almost but not quite pathless. When he first came across Loch Coruisk in 1936, WH Murray, that great sage of Scottish climbing, wrote "My wild dreams fell short of the wilder reality." My parents, on their visit at the height of wartime eight years later, clearly agreed. Loch Coruisk and its surrounding amphitheatre of barely accessible pinnacles seduces even those known for their love of other high places. "Nature's skyscrapers", AW Wainwright called the Cuillin in his book *Wainwright in Scotland*, adding in an implicit reproach of his own beloved, but more comely, Lakeland fells, that they were "the grandest mountains in all Britain". At Loch Coruisk, Robert MacFarlane writes in his book *The Wild Places*, time itself runs differently. The normal measurements – days, hours, minutes, seconds – don't apply. Even history loses its grip. Instead, the place "keeps wild time [which] finds its forms minerally and aerially, rather than on the clock-face or in the diary".

I'd been getting ready for the Cuillin all through my first year at Cambridge, building up my climbing skills to the point at which I was now rarely tackling anything less than VS (Very Severe). Whereas nine months earlier, I'd been taking my time with Count Henry over Hope at Cwm Idwal (135m, four pitches, rated Very Difficult), by Easter 1971 I was practically running up it solo in – according to my log-book – "10 minutes or so".

For nearly all of these climbs, my climbing partner was a slight, wiry, cherubic-faced boy from the Wirral with a great sense of humour called Gordon Taylor, who was reading engineering at Selwyn. We first climbed together on the sea cliffs of north Cornwall just before Christmas in 1970. At Easter, he came up to North Wales to stay at the cottage and we explored together a lot of the classic Welsh routes, and by now I was quite confident about leading. In June, the two of us climbed the Pel route on Castell Helen, a spectacular quartzite sea cliff on Anglesey, which involved two abseils down a 200ft vertical wall and only a tiny ledge between them. "Absolutely stupendous!" I recorded in the log-book – and why not: the second abseil ended on a small ledge just inches above the Irish Sea. All the climbing was with a backdrop of foaming white water crashing on the rocks below.

This was a time of learning, a time of firsts. After tackling Bow-Shaped Slab (VS) on "Cloggy" in 1971, I wrote that "I had never been so involved in a climb before: 100 per cent concentration." On the Anglesey sea cliffs, my first figure-of-eight abseil was followed by a reminder of what can happen if you do lose concentration, when we had to wait while a group above us traversed out of the way, having fallen and failed on the second pitch of The

Hustler, a spectacular continuous 130-foot corner pitch. As they retreated past, the leader commented that he thought the route harder than Cemetery Gates, a famous Brown/Whillans XS (Extremely Severe) route in the Llanberis Pass. It was a bit easier for us as we clipped the Moac nut which held their fall, giving us more reassurance on the crux move. It was part of my rack for years.

The very fact that I was keeping a log-book to record all these climbs rather than a diary was itself proof of my priorities: what mattered in my life back then was what routes I had attempted and how I had managed on them, not what thoughts I had about my life or what I wanted to do with it. All of that could wait. What mattered now were mountains, and being on them.

I don't think it really sank in at the time that my parents had taken us up to see the Black Cuillin exactly a quarter of a century after they'd first climbed them themselves. I don't know whether it was any kind of romantic anniversary, any promise that they'd made each other, as they swam in the cold seas in Easter 1944, that one day they'd come back 25 years later, married and maybe with children. The thought never struck me, or if it did, I thought nothing of it. Because that first sight of Skye, sailing up from the south in 1969, made the Cuillin part of my own personal mythology, never mind theirs. When you're a teen, you make promises to yourself like that all the time. *I'll come back here one day*, you say, and most of the time you never do. Only with a small and select group of places do you keep your promise. Skye and the Cuillins are such places for me.[4]

So it was that, at the end of my first year in Cambridge in June 1971, I headed there with Gordon and a few other CUMC friends. The bus dropped us off at Sligachan, just as it had done my parents before me on their 1944 trip. After walking to Glenbrittle we carried

---

4 I tried to pass on my love for them to my own children. Elinor and Owen – aged six and three – have swum in a cold Loch Coruisk just as their grandparents did half a century before. They've seen the bobbing heads of a score of inquisitive seals following our dinghy as I rowed them round. I hope their memories of the place are as magical as mine.

our food, tents and climbing gear up to Coire Lagain, where we camped for the week. On the first morning, we headed over the tops to Loch Coruisk.

> *Rarely human eye has known*
> *A scene so stern as that dread lake,*
> *With its dark ledge of barren stone . . .*

That was Walter Scott's description of Loch Coruisk in 1814, and when they read it in *The Lord of the Isles* (later brilliantly illustrated by Turner) his readers couldn't wait to see it for themselves. The fact that it was difficult to get to didn't put them off, no more than it deterred the boatloads who braved the crossing to Staffa to look at Fingall's Cave. And if Scott had first put Loch Coruisk on the tourist map, it was still firmly there over a century and a half later: on that first day of our 1971 holiday, I noted in my climbing log-book, a boatload of tourists landed at the top of Loch Scavaig. We saw them because I had wanted to revisit the anchorage we'd had the previous year on *Zuleika*. To get there we had climbed up to the ridge from our camp, down a frighteningly loose couloir to the headwaters of Loch Coruisk, then down to the sea, before returning to picnic at the foot of the Dubhs Ridge. Later on in this story, we'll come across the Dubhs Ridge again, but this was the only time I ever climbed it.

The verdict of the Scottish Mountaineering Club guidebook to Skye was, I discovered, spot-on: "There can be no finer way to the top of any mountain in the UK. 2000 feet of moderate climbing on good rock without serious difficulty." "It was superb climbing," I noted in my log-book, "with plenty of technical slabs to maintain interest." We pressed on to reach three peaks – Sgurr Dubh Beag and Mor and Sgurr Alasdair – and got back to the camp tired but happy after a totally satisfying ten hours of walking, scrambling and climbing.

We climbed a few other peaks on that summer camping trip in 1971 – I soloed up the Inaccessible Pinnacle (watched with incredible attentiveness, I noted, by seven other people) – while doing the ridge traverse of Coire Lagain. We saw Skye in all its many moods, from sunsets that turned the mountains behind us pink to continuous rain for a day after which the whole of the corrie ran with water. We had days when we could relish all the climbing challenges the Cuillin had to throw at us, with their mixture of gabbro (grippy, even when wet) and basalt (the opposite); days when the views were stupendous; and days when everything was lost to cloud and mist. We crisscrossed the imposing cliffs of Sron na Ciche, completing several of the 1200-foot routes of only moderately severe difficulty, and soloed to the top of that notable landmark, the Cioch. I got back home and tried to put what camping on the Cuillin had meant to me into words. "What an unforgettable series of experiences – both pleasures and horrors", I wrote. "And certainly, what must be one of the most beautiful and impressive settings anywhere."

By now, then, I was doubly hooked on this part of Scotland, this time because of its mountains as well as its seas. But just like my parents, I wanted to follow climbing the Cuillin with tackling the North Face of Ben Nevis when it was still covered in snow. In that wish, I was only following a link I found out about later. In the Coruisk Memorial Hut for climbers, run by the Junior Mountaineering Club of Scotland, there is a pine panel above the fireplace to honour the memory of two young men. The climbing hut was paid for by the parents of one of them and opened in 1959, six years after their son with his friend had been killed in an avalanche. It was built, the sign says, "to assist those whose sense of adventure, courage and good companionship finds outlet in the high hills".

And where were they killed, these two young men? They were in the most spectacular and challenging winter climbing arena that the UK has to offer, the North Face of Ben Nevis. Climbers come here from all over the world to pit themselves against the unique but often fragile snow and ice veneer which forms during the repeated freeze and thaw cycles of a typical Scottish winter. And I wanted to go to tackle its longest climb, Tower Ridge.

oooOOOooo

"It is noteworthy," wrote WH Murray, the great sage of Scottish climbing, "how often the red-letter days of our mountaineering come as a complete surprise." In his 1947 book *Mountaineering in Scotland* – a book my father thought so important that he bought me a copy even though he'd already got one for himself – that's the first sentence of his chapter on climbing Tower Ridge in Winter. But it's true – or at least it has been for me. And it certainly applies to the best day of my mountaineering life – the day we climbed Tower Ridge.

Tower Ridge. I have only got to think about it and Tuesday 14 March 1972 rushes back in pin-sharp focus. Because that's the other thing WH Murray could have mentioned about red-letter days on a mountain: they stay with you for ever.

Every serious climber in Britain knows Tower Ridge. On the north, gnarly face of Ben Nevis – the setting for so many other great routes – it is one of the longest climbs in Britain, soaring 600 metres to the summit plateau in a series of broken crags and rocky towers. Technically, it's not the most demanding climb you will ever find, but it still takes its toll – especially when plastered with snow and ice in winter, when its difficulty rating goes up by a grade – on the unprepared or the just plain unlucky. The sheer scale of the drop – about 1000 feet – beneath your boots as you traverse the Great Tower can turn your legs to jelly. Especially if you've never really climbed a demanding route with ice axe and crampons before.

And I hadn't.

So I knew even before I went there that the Cambridge University Mountaineering Club's President's Meet – to give it its full title – was going to be a challenge. What I didn't realise, as I woke up at 6am on a Sunday in the canteen at the bus terminal in Fort William and started walking towards the mountain, was how much the memories of everything that happened in the week ahead would come to mean.

First, though, I want to make a little digression. It's nothing to do with mountains, but it's everything to do with my love for them, and – I suppose – a little footnote about the times we lived in.

Whenever I look back on my mountaineering log-book, I can still just about imagine doing some things – a difficult layback, overcoming a nasty overhang, or that surge of adrenalin once I'd got to the top of a particularly demanding route. All of that and more comes under WH Murray's "red-letter day" heading. What I'm about to mention doesn't. Because this is the eminently forgettable side of climbing in the Seventies – getting to the mountains in the first place. For me and everyone I knew, that meant doing something we wouldn't dream of doing now. Hitching.

Sometimes – very rarely – everything would work out perfectly. That summer, for example, a friend and fellow CUMC member, John Hutchinson, and I had flown to Zurich to go climbing in the Alps. We'd hitched to about 20 miles outside the city, but night was starting to fall and the chance of getting to our campsite at Promontogno near the Italian border, a three and a half hour drive away, looked remote. Then along came a young man in a sports car and he actually dropped us off there. He was, he said, a conductor, and was clearly quite successful, although I never caught his name.

But my point is, most of the time it wasn't a matter of conductors in sports cars taking us precisely where we wanted to go. More commonly, our hitching journeys involved being crammed in a fish lorry driver's cab heading south from Fort William, or a van driving north, dropping us off among the drunks of Central Station in Glasgow in an eerily empty early morning city. Or six hours – six hours! – by the roadside in Invergarry on the road north to Mallaig (this was me trying to get to Skye) before giving up and going back to Fort William. Or (and this was me on the way back from Skye) setting off from Sligachan and taking 25½ hours to get back to Prestbury. Or how about these timings (this for coming back from Tower Ridge: 10am start hitching, Fort William; 8:30pm Carlisle and the M6; 1:30am Knutsford, and – because there never was a lot of traffic at that time – back home with a milk van at 4:30am?

I want you to think about all of those hours standing bored, by the roadside, breathing in exhaust fumes and sticking out an optimistic thumb at passing cars and lorries but really getting nowhere. Who, in an age when we didn't have a mobile phone to pass the time, would ever be prepared to waste hours like that, relying on the kindness of strangers to take us to the mountainous parts of the country? Yet that's exactly what we all did, and we thought nothing of it. And what does that tell you? Well, I'd argue, one thing. We loved mountains, we loved climbing so much that it made all the boredom worthwhile, all the frustration, all the dead time, all the six hours by the roadside in Invergarry, all the forced laughter at our drivers' jokes. All that dead time was worthwhile, because just for a few hours on a snowy peak, we lived so intensely that memories burn on into the present.

Talking of which, I should introduce you properly to Howard. I didn't know Howard Steen before Easter 1972. I might have seen him around Cambridge and at the CUMC, but neither of us knew each other well. Making us climbing partners was Mick Geddes's idea. Mick, Cambridge's second teenage prodigy climber, whom you met briefly in the last chapter, was the club's president in my second year. Along with Alan Rouse, his own climbing partner, Geddes would think nothing of hitching up from Cambridge to Fort William just to have another crack at Ben Nevis's snow-blasted northern face. Mick wasn't going to be there for that Easter 1972 meet. But he knew me – I was the club journal editor that year – from our informal weekly meetings and the eight or so talks by professional mountaineers that the club organised every year. And he knew Howard because they were both at Pembroke, both reading chemical engineering. Howard was especially helpful to Mick because every time he got back to Cambridge after another five-day weekend on a wind-blasted wintry Scottish mountain and needed to catch up with his work, Howard would lend him his notes. Mick thought Howard and I could be a great climbing partnership, and he was absolutely right.

On Sunday 12 March 1972, Howard had finished the last bit of his journey from Cambridge by hitching from Kinlochleven to Fort William and walking up to our meet at the Charles Inglis Clark (CIC) Memorial Hut halfway up Ben Nevis. But I'd got there first. I'd woken up in the canteen at the Fort William Bus station and set off for the Ben at 6.30am, just as the skies were beginning to lighten over the mountains to the east. Walking up with a heavy pack, it took me two and three-quarter hours to get to the hut, every step towards the end making me realise how unfit I was. But as the dawn came up on a cloudless sky and Ben Nevis loomed pure white 2,000 feet above (apart from her most monstrous icy crags) I met a climber coming down the track. He'd pulled a muscle and couldn't join the rest of his friends on the mountain. And that, he said, just made him sick, because after a lifetime climbing the Ben, these were about the best conditions he had ever seen: clear and bright, but not thawing, and all such a massive contrast to the rest of the winter, which had been horrendous.

Instead of waiting for Howard (remember: no mobile phones – who could possibly know what time he'd arrive?) I headed out onto those white slopes by myself. I was a bit self-conscious about my climbing gear: this was the first time I'd worn crampons and I was still desperately trying to avoid falling over them. And while climbers like Alan Rouse and, for that weekend anyway, his climbing partner, Rab Carrington had the new short Chouinard ice axes that allowed them to positively pelt up the slopes, mine was still too much like the old-fashioned, longer-handled axes. Even though I'd just had it shortened and the pick bent back at Ellis Brigham's climbing shop in Manchester, it still wasn't the real deal. Then again, maybe I wasn't either. We'd soon find out.

In that rare, seemingly safe, sunny Sunday afternoon, I headed out and up Ben Nevis's No 4 Gully by myself – my first ever "serious" snow route – and one that offered a certain amount of tension on the left wall near the top. Then I was up and on the summit, with the Mamores looking positively alpine to the north and a wonderful walk across the Carn Mor Dearg Arête to make me realise the sheer luck of being in the right place at the right time.

oooOOOooo

That Easter, I began a friendship with Howard that has lasted ever since. At the start, it might have had something to do with the fact that we were both relatively new to snow and ice. There were others in the CIC hut that Easter – louder, more extrovert, alpha-male friends – who were already confident about their ability on ice. But we weren't. When everyone said that we were all doing an alpine start the next day – up in the darkness of night and out on the mountain and climbing with helmet lamps long before dawn – well, neither of us had ever done that before.

But look at what Howard and I did have in common. We were both engineers and both, it turned out, pushed along that path by engineer fathers. We were both northerners by birth (or at least Howard was born in Liverpool, though his family had moved to Birmingham when he was seven), both 5ft 8ins tall, and both had a similarly solid build. Neither of us liked ball games but did like more individualistic sports: Howard was a judo brown belt and captain of judo at Cambridge while I was a modern pentathlon half-blue. Howard was also a half-blue for judo. We both had ordered, logical, unflustered minds, and yet we had a strong feeling for the natural beauty of landscape – we both liked photography but Howard was also a gifted artist and had brought his sketchbook along too. As the climbers came in off the mountain into the hut, draping their wet socks and climbing gear over the stove pipes, sitting around and talking about the day's exploits or preparing for an early evening fry-up, Howard was trying to get it all down on paper.

A climbing partnership goes a lot deeper than shared interests or mutual regard. You have to be almost exactly at the same level of ability, and we were. We were both using ice axes and crampons for our first big climb. But more importantly, we soon learnt that we could trust each other. That's the most essential thing on a mountain – to know that your partner is handling the rope correctly, that they are securing you when you need it and vice versa. And trust is easier if you are at the same level of ability, so you can agree on routes with the same level of ambition, and neither of you feels they're being pressured or over-faced. In that sense, emotionally as well as physically, climbing friendships are all about balance.

Right from the start, I felt that with Howard and I know that he felt that with me. We weren't, either of us, the kind of top climbers trying to push the limits of what was achievable in terms of clinging onto vertical or overhanging ice walls. Instead, we were just beginning to get into the sport and it still had all the excitement of discovery.

Tower Ridge suited us perfectly. We had both felt excited, looking up at that huge amphitheatre above the hut, trying to imagine ourselves up on those gargantuan snow and ice encrusted cliffs towering above us, or making our way past those cornices on the summit. That night, we crashed out at nine o'clock, and went to sleep wondering what tomorrow's climb would be like.

The alarm went off at five, echoing throughout the hut. Some people tried to sleep on, their bodies telling them that it was still pitch-black outside, so it couldn't possibly be morning and so they could still sleep on. Then someone heaved themselves out of their sleeping bag, pulled back the shutter on the hut window, and looked out. And there it was: a starry sky, a still, black night, cloud-free and likely to be cold. Good climbing conditions, in other words. Primus stoves were lit, porridge was made, and we started getting together ropes, crampons, axes, a few pegs and other paraphernalia of climbing gear.

Then, about an hour later, out we went into the starry night, the snow crisp and crunching under our boots, crampons biting well into the slightly icy surface as we headed up towards the North Face, towering up above us in darkness, silhouetted by the starry sky, and eventually to the bottom of the ridge. From there we roped up, took a belay to the top of the Douglas Boulder and then edged upwards along a narrowing ridge. The exposure was immediately obvious, the ground falling away on both sides and, to our left, the hut slowly diminishing in size at the bottom of the valley. Further along the hillside, you could see the waving head-torches of some of our friends heading off on different climbs.

By now it was about seven o'clock. We inched up the narrow arête. As the black sky slowly turned to a breathtaking blue, the sun started to rise and a pink glow spread up the snowy slopes.

Then the first serious pitch. The rocky rise up to Echo Wall was icy, and I led a pitch I was quite pleased with, getting a few runners in for protection, then onwards and upwards as the daylight flooded in. As we reached the Great Tower, we caught up with a couple of climbers who had been ahead of us. They had already put a rope around the Great Traverse on the Great Tower. The exposure here was absolutely awesome, with a thousand feet down to Tower Gully below. We very happily tied on that rope and went third and fourth on it.

The weather had been worsening all the time. There was so much snow on the steeper rock-steps which had become precarious and required a lot of cleaning. We managed to traverse beyond the Tower Gap and ended up on the ridge beyond it – which was great because it meant we then didn't have to face the hurdle of the gap itself. Then on to the cornice and the final ridge, and over that onto the plateau.

On the top, we were in a white-out. Ben Nevis is surrounded by cliffs on three sides and it is this that can kill people: when your whole world turns white and you forget which way you were facing, you walk towards what you think was the summit and you end up striding confidently onto a cornice which drops away and sends you plunging a thousand feet. We knew all of this, and yet those fears couldn't even begin to eclipse our feelings of euphoria. Howard got out his hip flask and we had a dram to celebrate.

OK, we hadn't followed the route as exactly as we had intended. True enough, we'd had a bit of luck coming across the other two climbers when we did, so the eastern traverse across the Great Tower hadn't taken us so long. No matter: we could always come back for a "clean" attempt and, when we did, we would be strengthened by the confidence that we had already completed a classic climb. Granted, we'd had a few strokes of luck, but all the same had climbed Tower Ridge in six hours, which wasn't bad: even the great WH Murray had taken seven. The previous day, we'd polished off Castle Ridge in as little as 90 minutes.

We walked in circles for a while on the 100-acre plateau at the top of Ben Nevis before the clouds lifted to show the Cliffs of Carn Dearg and a rock pinnacle we identified as the top of No 3 Gully. From then, we walked along until we found the marker post for No 4 Gully and made our way back down to the hut.

There's no feeling of contentment quite like the one you have when coming back after a challenging climb. All of its pitches are still fresh in your head, and you replay them together with your climbing partner, this time free of the adrenalin surge yet still seared into memory. You'll always have those memories, no matter what happens to you, and so will your climbing partner, whatever happens to him.

Howard and I got on so well that we both knew we'd go on a lot more climbs together. Later that year, we climbed in North Wales and Anglesey; the following year we climbed in the Alps around Zermatt and in Chamonix. Even after we'd both left Cambridge, we still kept in touch and went on climbs together in North Wales, the Peak District and in Scotland. Yet none of our subsequent climbs reached that pinnacle of perfection which we had glimpsed at while climbing on Tower Ridge.

Climbing partnerships are a very special kind of bond; one that is not easily replaced. I can't say I really thought about whether Howard and I would still be climbing together when we were both in our sixties; in your twenties nobody ever thinks that far ahead. If I *had* thought of who I would be climbing with in my sixties, I'd have certainly thought of Howard above anyone else. I enjoyed climbing with him and hoped that we would be climbing together as long as we possibly could.

Why ever not?

All too soon, I found out.

oooOOOooo

Chapter 5

A Change of Direction

St John's isn't the biggest or the oldest of Cambridge's 31 colleges but it has still managed to educate ten Nobel prizewinners, seven prime ministers, 12 archbishops, three saints and at least two princes. Along with that lot, in the 1970s, it also let loose about 25 would-be engineers on an unsuspecting world every year. In 1973, I was one of them.

Dad, Mum and my younger sister Diana – soon about to go to Cambridge herself – drove down from Cheshire for my graduation ceremony. My father complained that I should at least have had a haircut, and true enough it may have been beyond collar-length, but a sizeable number of graduands had centre-parted locks flowing halfway down their back, as if they had turned up for a Status Quo concert, so I reckon my parents got off quite lightly by comparison. The graduation ceremony in the Senate House was as dull as you could imagine, largely because it was all in Latin. Still, parental pride would have powered them through it. All they had to do was wait a while and at some stage their little darling would walk across the stage, bow in front of the Vice-Chancellor and then walk off through the Senate House Doctor's Door to receive his degree certificate. Meeting my family outside, I took it out from its scroll holder and showed it to them. I now was a BA (Cantab) Engineering Tripos Class 2 (ii). The big question was: what on earth was I going to do with it?

In truth, that question had been gnawing away at me for all the three years I was at Cambridge. Even when I first started, I'd begun to have my doubts about studying engineering. Although I knew how lucky I was to have all my expenses covered by my Rolls-Royce scholarship, for at least some of the months I'd spent in their Derby factory, I'd been frankly rather bored by the work. I'd enjoyed leading the project to build the illuminator from scratch – I could see the fascination of collective inventiveness – but too much of the rest of the work seemed repetitive, undemanding, and dull.

Then there was the Cambridge course itself. As kind people say in break-ups, "it's not you, it's me." In all three of my years at St John's, I seem to have spent endless hours in my rooms poring over problems without making any progress. Maybe that was just me, not the course, and I gradually accepted that. But while if I had done almost any other subject, those hours spent not coming up with answers to engineering problems could have been spent acquiring useful knowledge, in engineering those hours taught me nothing other than that I was studying the wrong subject. *It's not engineering*, I would have liked to have said, aiming for a painless break-up. *It's me.*

To my father, though, this was deepest, darkest heresy. No man in the country was more committed to the cause of promoting engineering at universities. Everything that I had done at Rolls-Royce – getting practical experience of engineering by working in heavy industry and, almost at the same time, getting a theoretical grounding in the subject at university – was almost a template for what he wanted to see happen across Britain. For me to turn my back on engineering was rather like the Archbishop of Canterbury finding out that his son had become a convinced atheist.

I may have disagreed with him back then – and we had a number of arguments whose bitterness I now regret – but I owe it to him to explain his side of things. I think if you'd have asked Dad what was going wrong with Britain, he'd have said that it was really quite simple: we'd stopped making things and designing things and being as inventive as previous generations. There were a whole load of reasons why this had happened, and he'd come up against a lot of them in his career. The bottom line, he'd say, is what do we value most? People studying, say, law at a place like St John's – like all the next generation of barristers, company lawyers and solicitors he'd have seen trooping out of the Senate House at Cambridge along with me on graduation day – or inventive scientists with no ties to the Establishment at all? Bankers in the City of London or engineers who could, perhaps, fire up the production lines at British Leyland? Manufacturing or the service sector?

Well, we know the answer, don't we? Or at least we know where the money was going, and it was flowing into the City and services and away from manufacturing. And because that's where the money was going, that's where people wanted to work. Against that tide, in his own way, Dad was trying to lead a fight-back. He hadn't given up on the idea of British engineering, on everything he saw at Metro Vicks in the Second World War. Engineering could save Britain yet. All it needed was a different way of being taught at university. A way that could scoop up bright talented kids (just like he had been) and give them jobs that industry needed. What there ought to be, he realised, was a link-up between industry and the universities that helped the one benefit the other. In 1974, the very year after I graduated, he co-founded the first Teaching Company Scheme in Britain to give potential engineers a similar mix of theoretical and practical training – "learning by doing" – that medical students get. These days, we call them Knowledge Transfer Partnerships, and they are now Europe's leading programme helping businesses (now no longer just engineering ones but almost every kind there is) to improve competitiveness and productivity through collaborating with universities and colleges.

In trying to establish links between industry and universities, people like my father were ahead of their time. The Science Park at Cambridge, for example, is now considered one of the most successful in the country, yet the first company only moved onto the site in 1973. A full five years earlier, at Salford, my father had persuaded the university to set up an Industrial Centre specialising in engineering design and manufacture. At the time, this was looked upon by the university with a lot of suspicion, yet as the Centre's chairman for the next 14 years, Dad saw it grow into a multi-million-pound business and possibly one of the reasons why in 1987 the government chose Salford as the site for the National Advanced Robotics Centre.

Back in 1973, all of this was impossibly far ahead in the future, and I only mention it to show the clear and coherent direction my father thought the future would run. But his path, I had already decided, wouldn't be my own.

Nearly all of my fellow engineering students seemed to be sharing the same kinds of doubts about careers in engineering. Of the 25 or so I knew, I can only think of three who took it up as a profession. This, to my Dad, would have been a killer statistic: if you want to know why the country's going to the dogs, he'd say, the answer's right there.

As for the rest, half were successfully wooed by the big accountancy firms, a few went into the Army or went abroad with NGOs. I signed up to be a graduate trainee at the merchant bank of SG Warburg & Co. I was there for 18 months, and although I was reasonably good at my job, I hated it.

Why? Maybe because one thing my father had taught me was that a job should be something you had to care about. Perhaps he cared too much: certainly that's what my Mum thought, and friends who came to stay for weekends but who never saw him because he was locked away with his papers and problems would have agreed with her. It can't be much fun being married to a workaholic, they probably went away thinking. But somehow in the back of my mind, I knew that I wanted to do a job that engaged me a lot more than doing the boring groundwork of preparing for a company flotation at a merchant bank. I wanted a job that absorbed me every bit as much as engineering absorbed Dad, and I knew that I would never find that working in the City, no matter how much money they threw at me.

My girlfriend Sarah – we'd met at the start of my final year in 1973 and married a year later – wasn't doing what she had studied at Cambridge either. Having studied history and religious studies at Girton, she was now training to be a social worker. We'd bought a run-down three-bedroom maisonette, 214 Boundaries Road in Balham (back in 1974, it cost a mere £8,500; these days the average price for a house there is £819,214) but whereas she started each working day with the positive attitude of someone who couldn't wait to learn more about her new job, I felt the opposite.

Have you ever been in the wrong job? If you have, you'll know all about that dead feeling you have inside when the weekend ends and Monday morning comes around again. And you'll also know how far you'd be prepared to go not to have that feeling, and to be able to get your life back on course again.

Even in my first year at Cambridge, I secretly wished that I'd studied medicine. That feeling now grew into a conviction. I applied to study medicine as a post-graduate, and I was accepted for a two-year pre-clinical course by two places – Bart's and the Royal Free Hospital. There was just one problem. I needed A level Chemistry and O level Biology. And I needed them both, starting from scratch, in just two months.

I resigned my job in April 1975, enrolled in a revision course for Chemistry A level and at a nearby technical college so I could do the practical chemistry exams. For the rest of the time, I was back at 214 Boundaries Road, head down and getting my brain around the periodic tables, organic and inorganic chemistry, learning the difference between electrophile and nucleophile, how to draw isomers and skeletal formulae and how to convince the examiners that I knew all about stoichiometry. It wasn't easy.

In the wider world, Saigon was falling to the Viet Cong, and in a referendum Britain was voting to remain in the EEC (67 per cent voted Remain). I paid no attention to any of that, working my way through the revision course at home and did about eight practical chemistry sessions at the technical college.

I needed an 'A' in the Biology O level and at least a 'C' in Chemistry A level. A 'B' would get me in at Bart's. A 'C' would do for the Royal Free.

In June 1975, I sat the exams and waited to learn my future. A month later, an envelope flopped onto the mat of our Balham maisonette. I'd got an 'A' in Biology O level and – to my enormous relief – a 'C' in Chemistry. I'd start at the Royal Free in September.

I was going to be a doctor.

oooOOOooo

Chapter 6

Wading through Treacle

Sometimes it is only when you look back that you can recognise the day on which your life changed forever. At the time, you wouldn't have known anything had happened at all.

Take my first day back in Cambridge, in September 1977. Finally, I was back in my old university, seven years after I had arrived as an undergraduate, this time studying the subject I wish I had done from the start. I'd completed my first two years of medical studies at the Royal Free Hospital but wanted to finish off by taking the recently introduced clinical course at Cambridge. The university insisted on my completing a further year of pre-clinical studies (Part IIb of the Tripos). That in turn meant meeting my director of studies at the beginning of term, who would tell me about my lecture programme and clinical supervisors for the coming months. A purely routine meeting.

It felt good to be back, not just in Cambridge, but at St John's. I walked past the Porters' Lodge, through three courts, and crossed the Bridge of Sighs, the covered bridge over the River Cam that Queen Victoria loved above anything else in the city. Just six years earlier, after the annual dinner of the university climbing club, I had climbed across it on the outside – not a particularly demanding climb, but I gained extra kudos from being able to manage it when the club president couldn't.

The Bridge of Sighs leads over to New Court, which is only new if you regard 1831 – when it was built – as recent. St John's is one of the larger colleges in Cambridge, and its buildings are spread over nine different courtyards. I'd lived in three, but easily my favourite were the rooms I had in my final year in New Court. 12A New Court: I remembered it well. How many undergraduates' rooms could compare to what I had – my own bedroom, kitchen, sitting room and bathroom, a view of the Backs, with trees all around, and all in a pre-Victorian building that was so much of a Gothic fairy tale, what with its towers, cloisters and crenellations, that everyone in the college knew it as "the Wedding Cake".

Dr Leake's room was three floors up a staircase across the court from my old rooms. He was a kindly man, with wavy hair and thick rimmed spectacles, and he told me everything I needed to know about my studies in the coming term. I thanked him, and went back down the stairs.

Actually, I ran down them, taking those polished stone steps four or five at a time. No reason. But suddenly, I slipped and landed on my backside. It didn't hurt, so I picked myself up and walked back over the Bridge of Sighs to the friend's flat in which I was staying. I can't remember what we did that night, I can't even remember the date – although it must have been either 28 or 29 September 1977. Either a Thursday or a Friday. That's the day my life changed forever.

Except, I didn't realise that it had. I was fine for the rest of the day and it was only the next day that I noticed I was walking with a slight limp in my right leg. I still didn't think anything was wrong, but I saw a GP on the Monday just in case. He suggested it was possibly concussion of a nerve root from the fall.

So I wasn't worried, and when, over the next six to eight weeks, my leg slowly got better and I stopped limping altogether, I thought nothing more of it. A month passed.

But then, very gradually, and for no reason at all that I could think of, I started limping with the *other* leg.

That's when alarm bells started to ring.

My doctor referred me to a neurosurgeon who referred me to a colleague of his in London. Which is why, in January, 1978, I was on a bed that was being wheeled into a room at the Guy's-Maudsley neurosurgical unit in London.

I didn't count the number of austere, white-coated doctors in the room, and I can't remember too much of what they said. I can't remember exactly how long they took over me before I was wheeled back out again. But one sentence rings out in my head as clear as it was the day the consultant neurosurgeon said it in a private room afterwards.

"The diagnosis is multiple sclerosis."

A cold, clammy feeling rose up through my chest. I didn't really know anything about MS, just that it would probably involve wheelchairs and severe, life-wrecking disability.

He left me alone to my thoughts, which raced wildly round my brain. In fact they weren't thoughts so much as a string of questions for which I had no answers. How long had I got before I needed the wheelchair? How long had I lost from my life? What would that life be like? Could I even carry on studying to be a doctor? Was there any point any more?

I'm a practical sort of person. I like knowing where I stand. When I'm on a boat, I love being able to chart a course, to work out where the obstacles are and how to avoid them. It's the same with climbing, and working out the best route up a cliff face. I can't stand uncertainty, yet in that room in the neurosurgical unit, I was faced by nothing else. My future was nothing but an enormous question mark.

I needed to get out, away from the hospital. Home.

Sarah drove round in our Morris Minor to pick me up. She had brought my sister Diana with her. "We'll get through this, Roger," she said, giving me a hug. "We'll get through this."

Bless her. But would we?

oooOOOooo

I didn't realise it at the time, and even if I had, it would have hardly cheered me up, but I had been diagnosed far quicker than most people with MS were back in the 1970s. Then, the average time from a person's first symptoms of MS until diagnosis was a full seven years: for me, it had only been four months. A technological revolution that would transform this situation even further was about to transform medicine. The first Magnetic Resonance (MRI) scan of the brain of an MS patient – the standard way in which the disease is diagnosed these days – was still three years away. But by the end of the 1970s treatment trials on disease modifying drugs for MS hadn't properly begun, the type of white blood cell that causes the actual damage to the myelin nerve sheath hadn't yet been identified, and a whole host of new therapies still hadn't been discovered.

If the science wasn't yet in place, neither was proper patient support. True, the MS Society already had 240 branches and 30,000 members, but it would be another 13 years before they introduced their excellent helpline (Tel: 0800 800 8000) and of course there were no internet support groups. People who were told that they had multiple sclerosis could expect to hear the devastating news as I did, straight after being wheeled into a roomful of white-coated strangers.

The irony wasn't lost on me. Only a month or so earlier, the neurosurgeon in Cambridge to whom my GP had referred me, had asked whether I would object to being discussed as an example of someone with Brown-Sequard syndrome, which is one of the consequences of the damage to the spinal cord caused by MS. That was the last thing I wanted. Ever since it was even suspected that I had MS, I've never wanted to be defined by the disease. Being stared at by all my fellow students as an example of it? I don't think so. Mercifully, he understood without me having to spell it out.

All the same, it wouldn't be too long before I myself was in a similar situation to those doctors gathered around my bed at the Guy's-Maudsley neurosurgical unit. Within a year, I would be starting my two-year clinical training on the wards of Addenbrooke's Hospital in Cambridge learning from consultants what a particular condition looked like and what were the signs to watch out for while making a diagnosis. I had already spent my first two pre-clinical years at the Royal Free Hospital (not at the ultra-modern Hampstead hospital which had opened in 1974 but in the old Medical School in Hunter Street, off Russell Square). Far from being swamped by learning all about the science of how the human body worked – physiology, biochemistry, anatomy and so on – I found that I actually enjoyed my studies. As well as studying, I completely renovated our maisonette in Balham. Looking back now, I can hardly believe that I had the energy to do all of that; then, I thought nothing of it.

Even though the diagnosis was made in London, it was Cambridge to which I returned and where I first came to terms with MS. Fortunately, there were some people there who had an inkling about what I was going through and who profoundly helped me. And because I never forget kindness, I shall never forget a consultant neurologist at Addenbrooke's Hospital called Mike Yealland – sadly, no longer with us – who probably helped me more than anyone else when I was at my lowest.

He was a tall, thin, bushy-eyebrowed, slightly stooped medical man of the old school – indeed, he'd been at Addenbrooke's Hills Road site since it first opened in 1961, when it was East Anglia's first neurosurgical unit. He was clinically brilliant, courteous to a fault, somewhat avuncular but never patronising, and always thoughtful and impeccably polite. These days MRI scans have become so quick and commonplace – nearly 50 million worldwide are done each year – that there is a natural temptation for neurologists to rely on the technology rather than their clinical skill or their ability to talk things through with their patients. This wasn't Mike's way.

He was already into his sixties when I got to know him. He had emphysema, but it didn't stop him smoking, and I can still remember how he would open the window of his office in the hospital when he had finished a cigarette and stub it out on the windowsill. Even more, though, I remember how he put me at ease at a time when I was completely on edge and fearful. We'd talk about sailing, because we'd got that in common. He and a friend shared ownership of a Hillyard 32 which they kept in Plymouth. In 1970, my father had chartered one for our two-week family holiday. We had sailed along the south coast before crossing to Cherbourg and Omonville in Normandy, and so I knew what a sea-kindly boat she must have been. But even if I had never been on a yacht in my life, it wouldn't have mattered: Mike Yealland had the open, reassuring manner of the very best kind of medic. He seemed to be completely focussed on helping me, and I never got the feeling that he wanted to hurry me out of the door and deal with another patient's problems. Just the opposite: whether he really did or not, he gave me the distinct impression he had all the time in the world to help me.

In his Cambridge hospital office, my own future stopped being a nightmare and started to fit together again – not admittedly in the shape I had always thought it would, but at least in a way I could bear. "Keep optimistic, Roger," Mike would say. "I have seen people in just as bad a way as you are right now go on have very fulfilling medical careers." And he was right. That's just what I have done.

I did try to keep in touch, and whenever I was in Cambridge I would often call round. One year, I did just that. His wife opened the door and told me that he had died a few months previously. My wife and I spent an evening with her and she gave me the old brass sextant he used on his yacht. It's in my study as I write this, a treasured possession and a particularly fitting one: an instrument to help sailors stay on course from a man who did just that for me.

oooOOOooo

That year, we sold our maisonette in Balham for twice what we had paid for it and moved into a Victorian terrace house in Earl Street, Cambridge. It's odd, isn't it, how you feel affection for some houses, even ones you lived in when things in the rest of your life might have been going wrong? Earl Street was like that for me.

If you really wanted to annoy anyone in Earl Street, you'd tell them that it looks just like Coronation Street. True, they are both front-garden-free terraced houses built to accommodate the Victorian proletariat, but there the resemblance ends. Back in 1978, our £27,000 bought us a three-bedroom house on three storeys, with a kitchen and shower room in the basement and a wood-panelled sitting room with an extension overlooking a walled patio garden. All in all, these days, it would set you back close to a million pounds. Not only was it a lovely, homely place, but it was marvellously located. Walk to the end of Earl Street and the lovely Victorian park of Christ's Pieces opens up in front of you. Stroll across that and the colleges are right ahead: Christ's, Sidney Sussex, and my old alma mater itself, St John's. In five years since taking my degree, I'd moved just half a mile. But I've always loved Cambridge, so that was just fine by me.

What wasn't, was what was happening to my legs. All the changes MS made were slow, but inexorable. At first, I would just have a slight limp, and though it would steadily get worse, I could only tell what was happening by comparing one week with the next. These "relapses" could continue for as long as eight weeks. Living with MS, I soon started to realise, wasn't just a matter of coping with the day-to-day problems it caused. That was bad enough. But the really frightening part of the disease was that I would never know how bad the cycle would get and whether or not it was going to take me completely off my legs.

The relentless certainty of that deterioration was bad enough, but those uncertainties were just as unsettling. I've always hated depending on anyone else, always been one to plan ahead, but with MS coursing through my legs, how could I? Would I, when my legs were getting worse, be able to hobble about on crutches, trying to get friends to give me lifts to the hospital? If they did, and someone else dropped me back, would it be one of those days when it would take me ten minutes to get from their car to the front door? I hated – absolutely *hated* – being seen like that.

Gradually, I would come to recognise when the disease's cycle was on the turn. Again, it wouldn't be anything I could measure from day to day. It might take six to eight weeks before I could feel my legs returning to something more like normal. But even though that would lift my spirits, always in the background there was the memory of how things were when the disease was at its worst and that it was likely the disease would return to affect a different part of my body within the next two or three months. On days like that, I would get out of bed and be unable to stand up. On the very worst days in the cycle, I could hardly drag myself out of bed.

I'm not, as anyone who knows me will testify, one for self-pity, but there were times in the next three years when I came close. I've already tried to explain how much climbing meant to me, about the complex joy of moving across rock with control and balance and safety. All of that was gone now. I've mentioned the cottage in North

Wales too, and how much that meant. It was just six miles from Snowdon, but my friends and I would think absolutely nothing of walking there and back – and even further – as well as a full day's climbing. It wasn't just the hand-holds and the foot-holds and the excitement of the climb that had been taken away from me: it was the walk-up as well. And the walk-back. And talking about it all in the pub afterwards too.

What made it all so galling was that I was 27 and ridiculously fit. Perfect eyesight and bodily co-ordination (aerobatics in the Chipmunk, climbing Tower Ridge with the CUMC, winning a half-blue for modern pentathlon) and back in a city with splintered memories of all three.

As far as my MS was concerned, none of this meant a thing.

When people ask me what MS is like, I often say that it's like wading through treacle. I've grown so used to it now that sometimes I almost forget what walking normally is like. The way you can switch off your brain, and let your feet move in a process almost as automatic as breathing, how you don't have to think about balance but how your feet pick up all the details they need about the ground you are walking on, and tell your brain all about it. And the motor signals to move will come straight back from your brain to your feet. *Move that right ankle just a little bit to the left so you can steady yourself. Make the toes on your left foot spring off the ground just a fraction harder than you normally would with the next step you take: you're going to need that extra lift because here comes the kerb and you don't want to trip up . . .*

Knowing where your body is in relation to both the ground and itself is a form of sensory feedback, called *proprioception*, a word which has been with us since 1906 when the science behind it was first worked out. Although the pathophysiology of MS is still being investigated, it is known that the disease process is one of inflammation and that this can affect any of the nerves in the central nervous system (CNS). It is the result of a nerve becoming inflamed that causes the loss of the myelin sheath (demyelination) and the nerve impulses not getting through. In a brain and spinal cord unaffected by MS and where the myelin sheath is intact, function should be normal in the absence of any other pathology. One's proprioceptive senses would be working and so walking is unthinkingly easy. But imagine if the nerve impulses, going to and from the brain, were not getting through (due to demyelination) then this would result in impaired function and inability to control and use the affected limb – a leg, for instance.

And that is what I mean by walking through treacle. Because those electrochemical signals from brain to feet can no longer be relied upon, walking becomes something you have to think about, a less certain, more provisional, process. When you can't take it for granted, this whole business of the bipedal, biphasic forward propulsion of the centre of gravity of the human body – walking – turns out to be more demanding and complicated than you'd think.

Why is the myelin sheath being damaged in the first place? That's the key question about MS and we're still far from knowing the answer. What seems to be happening is that the autoimmune system is attacking a perfectly healthy body, mistaking a perfectly normal part of it – in this case, the myelin sheath – for a foreign invader.

Because the autoimmune system attacks the nerve cells' myelin sheath in any number of different parts of the body, every case of MS is different, and this absence of clearly identifiable common symptoms used to make it difficult to diagnose.

The irony in all of this wasn't lost on me. Here I was, doing my pre-clinical studies in which I had to show I understood in detail the chemical and molecular basis of how cells and organisms work – and all at a time when my own cells and organisms were going so haywire that some days I could no more cycle to lectures to learn about such things than I could tap dance to Timbuktu. Neurobiology and Human Behaviour: that was another part of the Cambridge pre-clinical course. In my bleakest moods I thought: why bother learning about that? All they'd have to do would be to wheel me out on a stretcher in front of the class and they'd find out everything they needed to know: *Here he is, Chisholm RA, just another casualty of the "prime of life" disease. Why do they call MS that? Yes, you at the back. No? Because it most often strikes people in their twenties. And why is Mr*

Early sailing days on the Firth of Clyde with me on 'look out' duty. (1954)

The view from the rooms that I had in my third year, in New Court. (1972-3)

My Chipmunk at Marshall's Airfield, Cambridge, all ready and waiting to go. (1972)

At the bottom of the Dubhs Ridge, Skye. From left: Richard Pelly, Harry Cripps, Gordon Taylor, Roger Chisholm, Martin Hore. (1971)

With Howard, Kinder Scout. (1976)

Howard's sketch of some of the group at the CIC Hut, Ben Nevis. (1972)

Leading the way up Little Tower on Tower Ridge. (1972)

Making our way across the Eastern Traverse of the Great Tower on Tower Ridge. (1972)

The North Face of Ben Nevis (seen from Aonach Mòr), the most spectacular and challenging winter climbing arena the UK has to offer. (1974)

My photo of Howard on Monte Rosa with Lyskam behind. (1973)

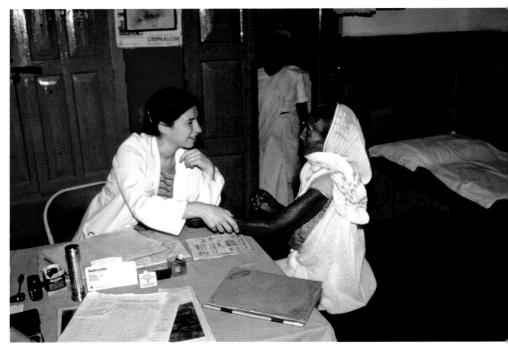

My sister Diana seeing patients in the outpatient clinic of Duncan Hospital. (1980)

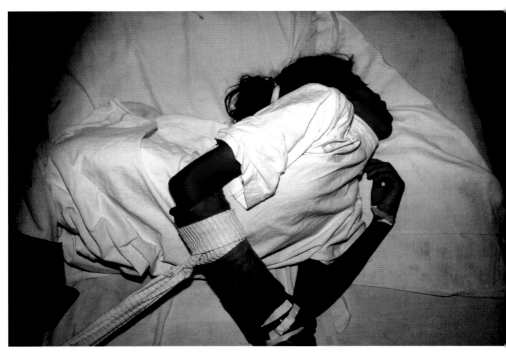

One of the tetanus patients at the Duncan Hospital. (1980)

Annapurna, Nepal (1981). I had wanted to see it ever since reading Maurice Herzog's best selling account of his ascent in 1950.

The mighty Macchapuchhare, Nepal – one of the most imposing peaks we saw on our 145 mile trek. (1981)

The best walk in the world. Crossing the Thorung La Pass at 17,769ft. (1981)

Climbing up from the Silvretta Hut to the Rote Furka Pass. (1985)

Chisholm here typical and atypical. Anyone? Yes, that's right, atypical because more women than men get autoimmune diseases; typical because more Caucasians get it than people with darker skin. Why is that? Don't worry if you don't know the answer. No-one has a clue.

In actual fact, people were very supportive. Mum, Dad, Di, Sarah, all my closest friends: everyone was kind and sympathetic and most of them gradually came to understand that though I appreciate thoughtfulness, I didn't want pity. It's a fine line and not everybody always gets it, but I think a lot of people with MS would understand.

I rang Howard, my old climbing partner, who was then working in Newcastle, and told him the news. He was shocked. All of a sudden, our time in July 1972 climbing Monte Rosa, the second highest mountain in the Alps, seemed a lifetime ago. If you'd have asked him back then which of us was the better climber, he'd almost certainly have said that he was better on ice but I had always got a much better sense of balance.

Balance? Now there was a cruel irony. One of the first things I had to get to grips with about MS was that you'd really got to pay close attention to your body to work out what was happening to it. Some days your sense of balance would be absolutely fine; a month or so later, it might seem to have gone for good.

Years later, I read about Saint Lidwina, a medieval Dutchwoman who enjoys the distinction of being the patron saint of both ice skaters and the chronically ill. In 1396, when she was 15, she was skating on a frozen river at Schiedam – now a western suburb of Rotterdam – when she had a bad fall. Afterwards, she had great trouble walking, but there were times when her symptoms disappeared altogether, and times when they returned. All of this is so similar to what happens with multiple sclerosis that some people claim she is the first known MS patient, suggesting that this was why she fell on the ice in the first place.

I have never yet prayed to St Lidwina, and it's probably too late to start now. But I can perfectly understand how miraculous that switch from being unable to walk to once again being able to do so. Even though I had fully absorbed that fateful diagnosis at the

Guy's-Maudsley neurosurgical unit, and even though, as a man of science, I accepted it, all the same I couldn't stop hope. There were times when, having been unable to walk, I would be shocked to discover months later that I could run. Then, optimism would flood back. I'd leave the crutches behind, and not even bother with the hawthorn walking stick my mother had given me, and which I usually strapped along the crossbar as I cycled from Earl Street to Addenbrooke's and back again.

But it wouldn't last. Another two months and the next attack would start. I'd try not to feel low and depressed, but how could you avoid it? This was a disease that took all your strengths and turned them against you. The healthier you were, the more your antibodies would rip apart the nerve cells' myelin sheath, and even though of course in the long run keeping fit and healthy is always going to help you, it just seemed so blatantly unfair. Sarah and I had been talking of moving to New Zealand to start a new life. Now that option was shutting down. Howard and I had talked for the last four years about one day climbing the great cliffs of the Lofoten Islands in Arctic Norway. That would never happen either.

I listened to Mike Yealland. He was a kind, good man, and he made me believe him when he said I wasn't to worry and I could still go on and lead a perfectly fulfilling life. Yet sometimes, as I suffered yet another MS attack, I'd ask myself who I was kidding.

oooOOOooo

Chapter 7

Flying a Three-Storey House

Demyelinating neuropathy, diplopia, internuclear ophthalmople-
gia: to someone who hasn't studied it, the language of medicine is
long, Latinate and off-puttingly opaque. But if all of these symptoms of MS might need translating for everyday use, there is at least
one which doesn't. The "useless hand syndrome". This is exactly
what it says it is. And of all the possible features of MS, it is not the
one that you want flaring up a fortnight or so before you take the
most important exam in your life.

To pass my finals, to be able to put the letters MB BChir (Cantab)
after my name and go out into the world and practise as a doctor,
first of all I had to spend four days being tested, both in one-on-one
"viva" interviews and in written exams about everything I had been
taught about clinical medicine during the previous two years.

There was just one problem. Because of the useless hand syndrome,
I couldn't write. True, I had some residual grip in my right (writing)
hand. I could have, for example, held onto to the handlebars of my
bike on which I cycled from Earl Street to the School of Clinical
Medicine at Addenbrooke's Hospital. But I couldn't hold a pen. No
matter how hard I tried, it kept flying out of my fingers.

You remember that word "proprioception"? Well, the useless
hand syndrome is a classic example of what it means in practice. It's
all there in the word's Latin roots: *proprio* (one's own/individual)
and "ception", from *capere*, to take or grasp. Your hand can still feel
things: if you brushed it with a feather or put it near a flame, the
reactions would be similar although less than for a normal hand.
What the syndrome takes away, however, is joint position sense and

that fine control over the hand's movements that we all take for granted while writing and for a whole host of other everyday tasks.

They put me in a different room to all the other medical students, gave me a Dictaphone to work with my left hand (useless hand syndrome rarely affects both hands at the same time), and let me get on with it.

Exams, of course, never tell the whole story about the person sitting them. They test acquired knowledge and – in the case of medicine – a doctor's capacity to apply it. Only indirectly, however, do they test motivation, or the reasons behind it, or fixity of purpose.

I'll explain what I mean. By the time finals rolled round, I knew exactly what kind of a doctor I wanted to be. Yet if you had asked me two years earlier, when I started my clinical medical studies, I wouldn't have had a clear idea at all. Back then – and in fairness, before I found out the hard way about useless hand syndrome – I had fantasies about being a surgeon. I could, I thought, put all my practical knowledge of engineering to good, medical use, fusing my existing expertise in mechanical engineering to my developing one in how the human body works. So: a career as an orthopaedic surgeon specialising in operations inserting artificial joints? Why not? I knew of engineer-surgeons who had done that.

I was still considering this when the time came to decide where to spend a two-month elective attachment. An elective is an attachment to an area in which the student wishes to gain further experience. Occasionally (as with me) it can also be the foundation of a subsequent career. At the time I was attached to a surgical firm (team) with consultant David Dunn[5] and he was offering a research-based elective. I expressed some interest in the elective to him but he replied "I don't really think surgery is a sensible idea for you." He said. "You're going to have enough problems in life without trying to hold down a surgical career too." This, I should add, wasn't a

5 David Dunn (1939-98) was a pioneer of endoscopic or "keyhole" surgery at Cambridge. He lived to see it recognised as a distinct surgical specialty and was made President of the Association of Endoscopic Surgeons in 1997. A keen rower, he also coached both the St John's VIII and Cambridge blue boat.

matter of Holmesian deduction on his part: I was in the middle of an attack of MS at the time and had hobbled into his office on crutches.

But Dunn wasn't the kind of person who raised a problem without also thinking of a possible solution. And his next words changed my life.

"You should meet Tom Sherwood, the new Professor of Radiology, who has just joined us from the Hammersmith Hospital. You should meet Chris Flower too. They both work in the radiology department here. In fact, that might be a good choice as an elective. Radiology is a very interesting speciality and undergoing rapid development both in imaging and interventional work. It is key to all the other specialities and you tend to see all the interesting patients in the hospital. I think you'd enjoy it." He set up separate meetings with the two of them, and within days I had met both and been accepted as the one medical student who would be taken on for an elective attachment in the radiology department between November 1979 and January 1980. And he was right: I did enjoy it.

It's no exaggeration to say that meeting Chris Flower and Tom Sherwood changed the course of my life. Now retired, these two people, who have been both mentors and friends, have been hugely important to me throughout my career. Thanks to them, I decided that I would attempt to specialise in radiology and become a consultant radiologist.

Not only are they important and inspirational figures in my own life, but they have played an important role in making Cambridge medicine what it is today. To explain what I mean, you need to see the Cambridge Biomedical Campus, the biggest in Europe. In its centre is the School of Clinical Medicine, which is now so large that it can offer a place (in year four) to everyone starting as a first-year medical student. And today's first-year medics would be well advised to stay on in Cambridge to do just that: if you quietly forget about Harvard, Cambridge usually tops the rankings for the best university in the world in which to study medicine.[6]

6 In some surveys it comes very closely behind Oxford but we won't go into that.

Just because the Cambridge University School of Clinical Medicine now enjoys such an impressive reputation, you might imagine that this was always the case but it wasn't. In 1973, when Chris Flower was appointed head of radiology at Papworth Hospital, Cambridge's School of Clinical Medicine didn't even exist. It only opened in 1975, and when it did, it didn't even have its own radiology professor. That took until 1978, with Tom Sherwood's appointment as the first professor of radiology in the university's 800-year history.

As medicine of some sort has been taught at Cambridge since a Benedictine monk called Godfrey arrived in the 11th century, and as degrees in the subject had been awarded by the university since 1540, the lack of a school of clinical medicine might seem like a bit of an oversight. The reason is that for centuries would-be medics at Cambridge had indeed been taught the "clean stuff" (the technical term for pre-clinical subjects such as anatomy, physiology and pathology) but they had gone abroad to for the "dirty stuff" (everything else) at universities such as Pisa or Leiden. In the 19th century, the London teaching hospitals took over this role. Cambridge medical students would go to London, amass all the clinical expertise they could, and then return to Cambridge to sit their final exams. The argument for doing things this way round was that doctors would see a far wider range of patients – and gain a correspondingly wider medical knowledge – in a bustling metropolis than in a smallish East Anglian city.

The arrangement seemed to suit everybody, so it ossified into tradition. Then in the 1960s, when the NHS realised that Britain needed more medical schools and East Anglia hadn't got one, it was decided to build one in Cambridge at the new Addenbrooke's Hospital, 2½ miles south of the city centre. This was the clinical medical school I joined in 1978.

Its success, though, wasn't assured. A lot of university medical schools were riven by rivalries between NHS staff and academics in the teaching hospital. In Cambridge's case, there was the additional complication of tradition: if the university's high-achieving students continued to choose London teaching hospitals for their clinical training rather than Cambridge's new medical school, the latter could be forced to close. By the mid-Eighties, hospital administrators were muttering darkly about doing just that. It didn't happen. The Cambridge colleges woke up to the realisation of what a massive asset they had on their doorstep, the school developed ever-closer links with a network of nearby hospitals, and fewer Cambridge students started finishing their medical training in London. The threatened axe never fell.

Part of that was down to people like Chris Flower and Tom Sherwood. For a start, they both liked and respected each other so there were none of the petty rivalries that bedevilled other teaching hospitals. Tom Sherwood became the Clinical Dean of the School of Clinical Medicine in 1984 and safely shepherded it through its darkest days. At Papworth and Addenbrooke's Hospital, Chris Flower made sure that the NHS in Cambridge kept abreast of all the latest scientific advances in radiology and pioneered new techniques that pushed the subject's boundaries even further: when I began my elective, for example, he was probably the only radiologist in the country doing flexible bronchoscopy, a technique generally within the remit of chest physicians.

I'd get to know them both a lot better when I came back to Cambridge from 1983 to 1988 to work as a registrar and then senior registrar at Addenbrooke's. But even those first eight weeks I spent in the Addenbrooke's radiology department for my elective, when I was given free rein to investigate everything going on within the department, was enough to convince me that I was making the right choice. Cambridge's School of Clinical Medicine was the newest and smallest medical school in the country but that had its advantages. Friends at the Royal Free in London would mutter darkly about how difficult it was when there were 20 medical students hovering around a bed to actually see the patient on whom they were being taught. In Cambridge, the patient/student ratio was significantly better.

On the September days in 1980 when I sat my final exams, alone with my Dictaphone in one room, about 75 other medical students were writing their answers down in the exam hall next door.

Seventy-five students: it might sound a lot, but it wasn't. With just 75 students a year, the Cambridge School of Clinical Medicine was barely viable. Now that most Cambridge students go there rather than to London, the danger of closure has long since passed. These days, it is so successful that the main problem is the number it has to turn away.

I got a 2:1 in my pre-clinical studies. For the clinical examinations there was no classification; the exam was a straightforward pass/fail. Despite the ferocious attacks of MS rolling into my body, I had still managed to work conscientiously over the previous two years. Even taking an exam with a Dictaphone, I had never felt out of my depth or under-prepared. Call me arrogant, but I knew I had passed.

I had prepared for this moment for a long time. I knew I was starting a surgical house job at Newmarket General Hospital in February 1981. Before that I had arranged to work for three months in a mission hospital in northern India and hoped to explore a part of neighbouring Nepal afterwards if my reduced stamina and strength could manage the 145 afterwards. I was going to live a little. I think I deserved it.

I booked a bucket-shop flight on a Syrian Arab Airlines Boeing 747 flight to Delhi, stopping off at Munich, Damascus and Dubai en route. Within a week of finishing my medical finals, on 9 September, I was getting up at 4:30am to be at Heathrow by 7am. On boarding the aircraft, I quietly mentioned to a stewardess that I had done some flying and asked if it would be possible to visit the flight deck at some stage. She said she would ask.

After we'd landed and taken off again from Damascus, the stewardess came back and said the pilot had no objection, and that I was welcome to follow her up to the cockpit. It was the middle of the night: most of the other passengers were trying to get to sleep as we flew on over the darkened Middle East. Once inside, I shook hands with the captain, an American, who indicated the empty co-pilot's seat to his right and invited me to sit there. I imagined that this would just be for a couple of minutes, but no: on we flew over the darkened desert, crossing into Iraq and down towards the Persian Gulf. Within a fortnight, Iraq would be at war with Iran, but at least for now the captain didn't have any altered flight plans to contend with as well as explaining to me which of the battery of illuminated dials in front of me and above our heads were the ones to which I really should pay attention. Another hour passed as we left Iraq behind us in the night, now flying above the Persian Gulf. With every passing minute, the captain explained, the plane was becoming lighter as more fuel was burnt, and as that happened, it tended to accelerate. To maintain a constant speed, he had to keep easing back the throttle.

By now it was 12:30am, and on the illuminated map in front of me, I could see Dubai getting ever nearer. We were going to land there in 20 minutes: surely now the captain would politely ask me to return to my seat? But – again – no. I would like to see what it's like to land a 747, wouldn't I?

There are days when life holds nothing but expectation. They are rare enough, but this was one of them. Already I had left Europe behind me for the first time, and was going to work in a hospital that would be vastly different from any I had ever experienced. And here I was, as the pilot gently lowered the nose of the 747 started our descent to Dubai, so gradually that the sleeping Arabs and Indians behind us wouldn't even be able to tell, seeing things I had never seen – those gas flares, scores of them, all the way to the desert's horizon, as we came in to land. As we finally came to a halt it felt strange to be so high above the ground – a full 25 feet, almost as if we'd been in an attic, flying a three-storey house.

It was 1:30am in Dubai. We'd reach Delhi at 6:30am. I had been in the cockpit for four hours already, and I'd be there for another two. Soon the captain applied power to the engines and we took off. Delhi awaited, straight on till morning.

oooOOOooo

Chapter 8

Doctor Sahib

I was tidying my study the other day when I came upon a small stash of letters from about ten missionary organisations running hospitals all over Asia and Africa, all dated about May 1980 and all turning me down for a job. I can't blame them: in their position, I'd have turned me down too. They were all looking for doctors who would be prepared to work with them for at least a year, and I had only got four months before I started my new job at Newmarket General Hospital.

Finally one arrived with a more optimistic response, and I secured a post at the Duncan Hospital in Raxaul, in the northern state of Bihar, right on the Indian/Nepalese border. They'd be getting a newly-qualified Cambridge doctor to help out at their 190-bed hospital, even if only for three months (I had plans for that extra month). I'd be getting a totally different experience of medicine from that provided in a British teaching hospital with its plethora of imaging and laboratory tests. I would also be exposed to pathology I'd never seen before. I wanted, for a short while, to see how doctors coped in that environment. To go back, as someone once said, to basics.

I looked up Raxaul on the map. The river flowing through it marked the boundary between India and Nepal – a country that had fascinated me for years. Only a generation ago, this was a mysterious Himalayan kingdom, closed to westerners. It was where, in 1949, my great hero, the taciturn explorer-writer, Bill Tilman made his last three mountain reconnaissance expeditions before he bought his boat *Mischief* and took up sailing instead of high-altitude mountaineering. For climbers, it was and is a deadly paradise, home to eight of the ten highest mountains on the planet – including, of course, Everest.

On 3 June 1950, the Frenchman Maurice Herzog became the first man to conquer one of those 8,000-metre Nepalese peaks. At the time, his team's ascent of Annapurna – at the first attempt, and without supplementary oxygen – captured the world's attention in the same way that Hillary and Tenzing's successful Everest expedition did three years later. *Annapurna*, Herzog's account of that near-fatal expedition – in which he lost all his fingers and toes – remains the best-selling climbing book ever written, with global sales of about 15 million. One of those copies was bought by my mother and was on our bookshelves at Prestbury; we'd all read it. My friend and former climbing partner Howard Steen's father bought another; after reading it, Howard determined to go to Nepal himself. He went with a couple of friends on a 20-day trek round Annapurna in October 1977. Although he invited me, I had just started my pre-clinical year at Cambridge and I was unable to join him; in any case, as I have already mentioned, I was showing the first signs of MS, even though a confirming diagnosis was still some weeks away. Howard came back enthusing about the awesome beauty of the Himalayan landscape and the friendliness of the people. It was easily, he said, the most impressive walk he had ever done.

MS or not, I resolved, I wasn't going to miss out on seeing the country whose border was only a couple of miles away from the mission hospital where I would be working. It might, I realised, be my only chance. In those days, employers tended to look askance at requests for holidays longer than two weeks at a time[7] so I didn't know for certain that I would ever again be able to take a four-week break from work. Either way, I wanted to use the time between finishing at Raxaul and starting at Newmarket as fully and enjoyably as I could, and for me that meant exploring Nepal. Even if it had to

---

7 Chris Bonington himself – in 1970 the first man to climb the south face of Annapurna – chose to resign from Lever Brothers so he could pursue more expeditions.

be on horseback, I was determined to see those Himalayan peaks. It would be absurd to be so near and not to.

So that, at least, was the plan as I stepped off the plane in New Delhi at 6:30am on 10 September 1980. I hadn't bargained on spending half the night in the co-pilot's seat of the Boeing 747 taking me there, but apart from that I was ready for everything that India could throw at me.

Or I thought I was.

One thing I wasn't prepared for, as I cleared customs and gradually got used to the heat and the crowds of Palam Airport[8] (just one terminal back then; there are six now) and walked out into the arrivals hall was to see my sister Diana waiting for me behind the barrier. Now that really was a surprise.

The last time I mentioned Diana, she'd come down to Cambridge with Mum and Dad for my graduation in 1973. Since then, she had graduated there herself after studying medicine at New Hall, and was working as a doctor in a small (20-bed) Prem Sewa Hospital[9] at Utraula in eastern Uttar Pradesh. It was great to see her, but totally unexpected: first of all, her own hospital was more than 400 miles away; secondly, it was 6:30am; thirdly, this was India, and anything that could go wrong with best-laid plans invariably did.

Diana had booked us into a squalid budget hotel in the Old City (although as she pointed out, it was at least central) near the Main Bazaar, so once I had got some perfunctory sightseeing (Red Ford, Masjid Mosque) out of the way, I wasn't too disappointed to leave the following night, when we caught the 21:30 train to Lucknow which – trust me – sounds a lot more romantic than it turned out to be. I spent the night on a luggage rack and found I had to take great care where I placed my feet when visiting the toilet. In fact, although I shared every other visiting westerner's incredulity at the sheer

8 It was renamed Indira Ghandi International Airport after the former prime minister of India, who was assassinated in 1984. Her son Sanjay was killed in 1980 when he crashed his plane while performing an aerobatic manoeuvre at a smaller airport in the city.
9 It was run by the same organisation which looked after the Duncan Hospital. I'd found work for both of us.

range of India's sights and sounds, it's fair to say that I didn't fall in love with it.

The reasons piled up in my notebook: the open sewers in the street; the blank-eyed druggy stares of the western hippies; the way the buses would stop a full hour in the baking sun and *only then* announced that they weren't going further; the stodgy food; the trains you'd see passing level crossings at night, all those shrouded faces on the coach roofs like passing ghosts . . . Everything about India in those first few days made me realise just how profoundly European I was. And, at times, how homesick. Worse, however, was to follow. I had no sooner arrived at the Duncan Hospital than I collapsed with a temperature of 102°F and repeated vomiting and diarrhoea.

Diana had accompanied me on the long 600-mile journey to the Duncan Hospital, and had shown me round her hospital at Utraula, which was about two-thirds of the way there. She seemed, I noticed, to fit into India rather better than I did, and was actively helping out at the Duncan Hospital. Officially, she was there to get as much experience in obstetrics as possible – unofficially, for those first four days she was looking after her sick brother.

After four days, I recovered well enough to help out in the out-patient clinic and the next day joined the ward round. The hospital, named after a Scottish surgeon-missionary, opened as a 30-bed clinic in 1930 and had diversified and grown ever since. A brick-built building in reasonably good state of repair, it was one of two small hospitals serving the rather nondescript town of Raxaul (population 60,000). The main crossing into Nepal was 400 metres away, but the Nepal it overlooked was a far cry from the country of my dreams. That lay about eighty miles further north, a long strip of white on the horizon. This part of Nepal was its boring industrial hub, and both it and Raxaul were on the hot, dusty plain from which those distant snowy uplands appeared like an unlikely mirage, shimmering in the haze. The railway junction was about 400 metres away too, the town centre (such as it was) about the same distance again. It was hardly an exotic destination so much as an uncomfortably hot Bihar Burnley, complete with mosquitos.

The hospital treated many diseases I didn't know much about – tetanus, mosquito-borne encephalitis, TB and leprosy among them. Of about 150 recent cases of encephalitis, half had died, although we still had one or two cases on the male ward for whom we could do little except be supportive. And that, I suppose, was one of the main things the Duncan Hospital taught me: that when there are limits to what is medically possible, it is still important to show you care. I remember people coming along to my bedroom at night, carrying a candle, saying: "Doctor Sahib, could you come along and look at this male patient?" and I would go along and do just that. There might have been nothing at all I could do. To add to my helplessness, I couldn't even speak the language. Yet one sensed all the same that it mattered to the patient that I had at least made the effort.

Every day, I would witness things I never would in a British hospital. I visited the local leprosy village with the only resident surgeon (a missionary doctor, trained at Guy's Hospital in London). I saw a number of his operations and all were carried out under either spinal anaesthetic or with the old EMO (ether) machine: there was no general anaesthetic capability. There was also trauma: as the result of a kukri (Gurka knife) fight one patient had his larynx and oesophagus half-severed, his skull cut and his hands almost split in two. As the surgeon pointed out, it was a wonder that he was still alive.

Many of our babies, however, weren't. The mothers would often come in with deliveries which had been obstructed for a day or more, in which case the foetus had usually died. We were doing far more craniotomies – a distressing operation in which the foetal skull had to be broken in order to extract the foetus – than any British hospital could contemplate. And while a special care baby unit in a British hospital would be able to anaesthetise and ventilate its new-born charges, on ours the parents would take it in turn to "bag" them (inflating their lungs by hand), sometime for days on end.

Patients came in with advanced tumours all the time, and there was nothing we could do for them. We would tell them this, and they seemed to accept it, turning to leave without saying anything else. I don't know whether seeing that level of resignation made me any more accepting of my own MS. By rights it should have done, but I have never been particularly good at being resigned to my fate.

The numb hand syndrome I suffered from was a good example. It hadn't gone away since I took my finals in Cambridge, yet for the previous week or so I had been painstakingly training myself to write with my left, or "wrong" hand. Try it yourself, and see how hard it is: your first attempts will look like a four-year-old's: uncontrolled, the individual letters all different sizes. Yet the more you practise, the more the letters even out: true, they might slope backwards at odd angles, but they gradually become recognisable as handwriting. I would never be anything near ambidextrous, but within a couple of weeks I was writing patients' notes with my left hand.

The great test of how well – or how badly – I could use my left hand wasn't long in coming. The hospital was about to hold an "eye camp" – a blitz on cataract surgery. It had been widely advertised and about 200 people had come in from a 50-mile radius. Doctors were all reassigned new tasks. I was given charge of the male medical ward for the duration. In addition I helped anaesthetise the eyes of the patients undergoing cataract surgery. This involved using my left hand to inject a rather blunt needle behind their eyeballs: a retro-orbital block as we doctors prefer to call it.

There's an old medical dictum – "see one, do one, teach one" – that tells you everything about how surgical procedures used to be taught (and sometimes still are). Its meaning is self-explanatory, but it indicates a wider truth about the practice of medicine: that there's no room for time-wasting fussiness: instead, you have to pay careful attention, roll up your sleeves and get on with the job. So it was at Raxaul: the cataract patients came in three at a time and would lie down on camp beds. At this point a medical student and I would perform the retro-orbital blocks, and off they would go into theatre. At Newmarket, I would never be entrusted with such a task with my "wrong" hand, and the only needles used would be disposable. Here, the needles had to be sharpened each time. It was medicine at its most basic, but it was fascinating. What I experienced in India has stayed with me all my life. It also reinforced my appreciation of just how fortunate we are with the medicine and facilities we all take for granted at home.

Sometimes, I catch an odd, fleeting memory. Of being bored in the half-hour Hindi sermon in the church on Sunday mornings. Of all the background sounds floating across from the town as I lay reading on Sunday afternoons: sirens cutting through the amplified wail of Indian music; the huffing and puffing of the so-called express steam train from Calcutta arriving at the Raxaul junction; and as darkness fell, the sound of children playing and fighting, mingling with occasional shouts and the relentless angry honking of cars and lorries. Wondering, as I lay there, what it would be like to travel over that so-near border, and head off to that cold, white horizon.

oooOOOooo

Chapter 9

The Best Walk in the World

Ask any truly seasoned traveller about the Annapurna Circuit, and they'll know exactly what you mean. It's a 145-mile walk in the Himalayas around a string of 23-26,000ft peaks, taking in not just one of the highest trekking passes on the planet but also one of its deepest gorges. Starting off in sub-tropical forests and paddy fields, your three-week walk will take you through implausibly steep-sided valleys up to the very edge of the Tibetan Plateau, where you may struggle for breath because the air has only half the amount of oxygen found at sea level.

But the views, too, are breathtaking: of the sun rising over range after range of serried mountains, of donkey trains making their way over rope suspension bridges over jaw-dropping chasms; of the snowy peaks of mountains bigger than you have ever seen, blushing pink in the sunset above darkening valleys. And it's not just an impossibly scenic walk; it's also a culturally varied one. As you head north and leave behind the Hindu villages of the lower foothills, the whole culture, religion, and architecture of the place start to change around you, becoming increasingly Buddhist. Even people's faces begin to look more Tibetan. Their tea-houses and homes – indeed, all of their buildings – change from being made of wood to stone, and you can see why as you look around you: those enormously tall pines and forests of rhododendron, oak and maple of the lower valleys have thinned away to nothing, the landscape has become barren, and trees more sparse. Wood becomes more expensive the higher you go and the more you need the warmth of a fire to keep the cold at bay.

Because the landscape *is* so spectacular and changes so markedly as you walk through it, the Annapurna Circuit is routinely described as the best walk in the world. Or at least it used to be, until the 21st century started to creep up its valleys. But we walked the Annapurna Circuit when that boast still held good, in 1980-81, when it still had no roads, when most goods were still ferried up its valleys by yak, donkey train and porters and not Jeeps and vans. We walked it before it was even known as the Annapurna Circuit, and we walked it the hardest way round, in January, one of the hardest months to do it and when the avalanche risk is high. All of that, and – in my case – with MS too.

That trek meant a lot to me. Before I explain why, I need to tell you a little more about the route. Imagine a map giving an aerial view of the landscape I've just described. It has no roads, just paths into the hills that have, all the same, been trade routes for centuries, with donkey, mule and yak trains up to northern Nepal and southern Tibet carrying rice and wheat and returning with wool and salt. Some of those paths can be joined together to make a circular route. That's all the Annapurna Circuit is, apart from the fact that it runs through such spectacular scenery. For those of you with extreme imaginations, it's about the same length and – very roughly – shape as the M25 orbital motorway round London, with which it otherwise has absolutely nothing in common at all[10].

After I finished work at the Duncan Hospital, I caught the bus north to Kathmandu, where I waited a day for Sarah to join me. When we first talked about doing this journey together, I couldn't be sure whether my legs would be up to the challenge as my MS relapse was still evolving: I therefore made a contingency plan whereby we could take a horse if I was unable to walk. I'd raised the matter with Mike Cheney, a former Army captain in his early fifties who had been base camp manager on Chris Bonington's successful ascent of the south-west face of Everest five years previously and

10 If you want to be toxically pedantic, I would concede that it is more of an oval than the M25 and there's a slight extension near Watford on its north-west but otherwise this non-comparison makes complete sense.

who knew Nepal backwards. He'd lived there since 1965 and had helped to set up its trekking industry. Concerned at the poor treatment many Sherpa guides and porters received, he set up and ran a company called Sherpa Co-operative Trekking. Howard had recommended them after his 1977 trek – he said their Sherpas had saved his life – so they were the company we picked too.

By 23 December 1980, when we met Cheney in Kathmandu to finalise the route, I thought my legs were working well enough for me to attempt at least the first day on foot. That's how we planned to make the journey: one day at a time. My right hand was still suffering from the useless hand syndrome I'd had for my Cambridge finals, but my legs seemed OK, and my stamina levels fine. "At the beginning of a journey," my hero HW (Bill) Tilman once observed, "one should, of course, be on fire to start, the feet tingling to tread the trail, the back itching for its unaccustomed load, a fierce contempt for motorcars uppermost in one's mind." Precisely.

Cheney introduced us to our Sherpa, Pertemba – think of a Himalayan Jeeves and you wouldn't be too far wrong – and we met again the following morning. On Christmas Eve, we made a five-hour bus journey west to Pokhara, walked an hour to the north and stayed overnight in a lodge at a village called Hyangja. After shopping for warm jumpers in the adjacent Tibetan refugee camp, on Christmas Day morning we set off.

We were at the most southerly part of the Annapurna Circuit, heading north-west up towards Ghar Khola and Kali Gandaki valley. This part of Nepal had been an established trekking route for the past 15 years. The route ran up the extended left-hand side of the oval – but back in the late Seventies usually ran straight back down again, because at the top was a pass which relatively few westerners attempted. Over that pass – the Thorong La, at 17,769 feet above sea level – lay the Marshyangdi Valley and the rest of the eastern half of the oval comprising what is now known as the Annapurna Circuit.

Back then, though, it wasn't – mainly because the Marshyangdi Valley was a "forbidden valley" that had only opened to westerners in 1976. If only we could get over the Thorong La, we could find ourselves in places tourism hadn't yet had the chance to touch. The Marshyangdi Valley had been explored by Tilman on his 1950 expedition on which he made his oh-so-near attempts on Annapurna IV and Annapurna II in 1950, when he was 52. It would, I felt sure, have hardly changed in the subsequent 30 years. The lure was irresistible.

I'd already told Cheney how much I wanted to go over the Thorong La and complete a clockwise circuitous journey back to Pokhara along the eastern valleys. He had understood perfectly. I forget whether or not he told me he had met Tilman, but he certainly knew one of the men who had accompanied him along those once-forbidden valleys on his 1950 expedition. In those days, Nepal wasn't properly mapped and Tilman was only allowed in by its king because he was ostensibly part of a small team of British diplomats and scientists. Its main mountain trails, and the passes they led to – even some of the most important ones – weren't even marked, so getting lost was easy, as the French climber Herzog had also found on the way to Annapurna. Wisely, Tilman had invited Jimmy Roberts, a major in the Gurkhas, to join his expedition because of his knowledge of the Himalayas and his ability to speak fluent Nepali. Roberts then went on to found Mountain Travel, the first trekking company in Nepal. Cheney worked for him for years and then went into business on his own.

The plan we drew up was simple. All depended on getting across the Thorong La Pass. That, in turn, depended on the weather. But there was another factor too. How, over the next 11 days, would my legs hold up? Would they be able to withstand a trek that would take me 2,000 ft higher than the highest peak in Europe, a full 2,500ft higher than I'd ever climbed even before I had MS?[11]

Pertemba knew the first part of the route well. In 1980, 19,000 westerners went to Nepal for trekking holidays, and although there were plenty of other routes (Everest, Langtang etc.), the trek up the Kali Gandaki Valley was especially popular.[12] Because tourism there

---

11 Howard and I had climbed Monte Rosa at 15,300 feet in 1973
12 By 2000, that figure had increased by 100,000.

was at least a decade old, there were plenty of lodges and tea-houses in which to stay en route. Hire a guide and a porter, and you could walk up the valleys in relatively easy stages and not at uncomfortable altitude. It was all eminently do-able – even, come to that, without guides and porters – and in December and January there would be no shortage of lodges in which to stay. So our itinerary was set: Hyangja, Khare, Modi Valley, Beni, Tatopani, Ghasa, Tukuche, Jomosom, Muktinath. That was almost as far as we could plan with certainty. Once at Muktinath – a pilgrimage destination for both Buddhists and Hindus – we would decide whether or not crossing the Thorong La Pass was feasible. If it wasn't we would return the way we'd come, stopping at different villages and maybe exploring a side valley. If that happened, I could still console myself that I was in Tilman country, this time following the Kali Gandaki river south on the first stage of its journey to the Ganges, where it flowed through the barren, mountainous northern valleys, as Tilman described it, running "at the bottom of a deep trench as if ashamed of hurrying stealthily by, withholding its life-giving water from so thirsty a landscape . . ."

Obviously, when we got to Muktinath, I wanted to push on eastwards over the Thorong La into the recently-forbidden eastern valleys, and so did Sarah. But that was up to the gods, the weather, and my legs.

As far as my legs were concerned, my stamina and strength seemed just about equal to the task in the early part of the walk. We could only hope that would continue as we climbed higher and the stages became longer. The second day – apparently the one when the guides get a sense of how difficult their charges are going to find the journey – passed off without incident. If anything, the walk up a flattish ridge to Khare struck me as fairly easy.

Gradually, we learnt what to expect. We'd reach the lodges every day at about 3:30pm. Down in the valleys, darkness fell a couple of hours after that. At the start of the walk, the sheer immensity of Annapurna South, Macchapuchhare and Dhaulagiri lorded it over the valleys, though as they narrowed we'd lose sight of them. When night fell, we'd usually eat dinner (lots of omelettes, vegetable fried rice, noodles, honey pancakes). There were, even then, quite a few other Europeans in the lodges, where at night there would be candle light or a paraffin lamp, but obviously no electricity or anything sufficient for reading. Toilets either didn't exist or were lamentable when they did. The worst I experienced was when I heard grunting and snuffling below the outside toilet seat where I was perched and, to my horror, I realised there were several pigs feasting on the excrement below. We missed a ready supply of hot water for washing even more, although Pertemba usually tried to get us small bowls of warm washing water at the day's end. At Tatopani, on day five, bathing in the hot springs beside a glacial river was sheer bliss, though you had to keep vigorously stirring the water to ensure you weren't either frozen or scalded.

In the mornings, we'd be served black tea in our rooms and often given a bowl of cold water to wash in. Breakfast was usually porridge, sometimes eggs, and we'd always be off before 8am. At each place we stayed, Pertemba would make sure we got the best room, insist on it being freshly cleaned, and that we were promptly served in the restaurants. Sometimes he went to sleep guarding our bags. Occasionally, he did the cooking.

I had a reasonable SLR camera, complete with new telephoto lens. There were so many things to photograph that I soon learnt to ration myself: one only needs so many photos of plumed donkey trains, tangerine orchards, rickety suspension bridges, small girls milling maize, waterfalls, yaks, children playing hopscotch, women weaving baskets spinning wool or de-lousing one another. A colourful store of memories all the same.

On this first, western half of the trek, we met quite a few Europeans who just seemed to be touring the world non-stop; others had jobs to go back to. At Tatopani we met two Americans who had come over the Thorong La the previous week. Worryingly, they talked about wading through knee-deep snow in freezing temperatures.

After a week's walking, we reached Tukuche, and the landscape became more barren and desert-like. The few villages we passed looked almost Arabic from a distance, sheltering beneath dusty cliffs. This was Buddhist country, with chortens and prayer wheels gradually, but not entirely, replacing Hindu temples, prayer flags flapping hopefully in the wind, and mani stones[13] alongside the trail often in places where spirits were thought to dwell even before the rise of Buddhism. That day's walking had been particularly long, my legs were starting to feel weak, and I had a temperature. I lay down on my sleeping bag and drank glass after glass of hot chocolate and rather than going down for dinner was grandly served vegetable omelette in bed. Perhaps, I felt as I went to sleep, I could do with some of those Buddhist prayers myself.

The next day was New Year's Eve, bright and balaclava-cold, with the wind from the north. The villages we passed were walled, the houses inside them flat-roofed and covered with earth, and huddling together on narrow, viewless streets. At Jomsom, for once we were in a lodge where there were no Europeans, and we both agreed we preferred it that way. Even though we couldn't speak a word of Nepali, it felt good to be welcomed into this Himalayan world and watch our hosts spinning wool by the fire or quietly chatting away as they cooked. After that, it felt rather disconcerting to be pulled back into modernity by cheery Americans in mirror aviator glasses or Australian backpackers who wanted to let you know exactly where on the lonely planet they'd been and how it compared to whatever they'd seen in Nepal.

Pertemba had arranged for us to have a new, stronger porter capable of carrying heavier loads: if we really were going to attempt the Thorong La in three days' time, we would certainly need one – and one with proper shoes on his feet too. Our departing porter had only gym shoes which were placed in plastic bags, bound around with string to provide some grip on slippery ground or ice – and warmer clothes. For one thing, there was now snow on the ground – powdery and not melting in the sun – a reminder that we were getting higher. Jomsom was 9,000 feet above sea level, Muktinath

---

13 Mani stones are stone tablets, rocks or pebbles inscribed with the mantra "Om mani padme hum" and created as a form of prayer.

12,171 feet. If we were going to get over the Thorong La, we still had more than another 5,000ft to climb.

Bill Tilman had come this way too, although not in winter. Compared to the barren plains, he wrote in his 1952 book *Nepal Himalaya*, Muktinath "appeared green and luxuriant, like an oasis in a mountain desert." The gods had smiled on the village in other ways too. First, its abundance of black ammonite fossils – worshipped by Hindus as shaligrams, or stone representations of Lord Vishnu – made it a holy place. And if the fossilised remains of ancient sea creatures so high in the mountains, so far from the oceans, seemed miraculous, what about the natural gas vents, which, when lit, produced flames burning from both earth and water? At the Jwala Mai Temple, here was indeed a sign from the gods. Fire from water? Such a thing was impossible except in a special place, a place worthy of pilgrimage. A place where devout Hindus would make their way up following the Kali Gandaki river, reach the end of the world, worship, and turn back down the valley, heading for home.

We were coming to the point at which we, too, would have to decide whether we were going to do the same. We had a rest day to think about it. Pertemba – who had spent the previous night trying to talk to a Japanese trekker who had come over the pass and was clearly absolutely exhausted – was convinced that it would be folly to do so, but agreed to go along with us on a recce. We climbed up the start of the pass for a couple of hours. Apart from a couple of 20-yard stretches on an icy traverse, I managed tolerably well. Sarah, however felt very weak, and so we went back down again. Maybe, I suggested, we should abandon the plan and instead explore a side valley we'd passed on the way. Not a good idea, said Pertemba: the valley was prone to avalanches in January, and a few years ago, six trekkers had died in one.

We could both see all the arguments against going over the pass. First of all, I still didn't know whether I could rely on my legs. Secondly, Sarah seemed to be having problems with the altitude. Third, the trekking books all said that the pass shouldn't be attempted in the direction we were crossing it, from west to east. There was a reason for that. The maximum "safe" altitude gain per day without danger of altitude sickness was 400 metres higher than the place at which one has slept the previous night. Just to get over the top of the Thorong La we were talking about four times that, more than twice the single-day height gain involved in going across the pass from east to west. No wonder Sarah had started to feel sick.

I certainly didn't underestimate the dangers. Three years earlier, Howard had told me about his ordeal crossing the Tilicho Pass ten miles to the south. He had picked up a stomach bug and had to leave the tent several times in the night in the freezing cold. That almost wiped him out, and he only got to the top of the plateau by virtually crawling the last few yards. He was, he said, in a strange kind of daze and without the help of the Sherpas he might not have made it. Afterwards, one of them told him he'd thought he was going to die. So no, I had every respect for the dangers of crossing the pass. I asked Pertemba what he thought. "You must think for yourself," he replied, "but whatever you like is OK by me."[14]

Back in the lodge, after visiting the "fire and water" temple (a bit of a disappointment: a blue flame in a darkened cave and the sound of running water – not, as we had been led to believe, a flame burning in the air above water) Pertemba obtained hot water for us and we washed before dinner. We talked again about going over the pass and resolved to try it, so Pertemba went off to find kerosene, firewood and food. A Canadian girl called Valerie attached herself to us, moving her bags to our lodge from the one at which she had been staying. She had met an English guy called Ron and said they'd be going over the pass together tomorrow too. We didn't wish to travel as part of a larger group, so while Pertemba arranged for our hosts to provide us with porridge at 4:30am, he also told them to tell Valerie that the earliest they could manage breakfast was 6am. We'd be long gone by then.

I couldn't sleep because I was psyched up for crossing the pass. Sarah couldn't sleep because she was too cold. We would, we agreed, let the weather decide for us.

14 The dangers of the Thorong La Pass were further and tragically underlined on 17 October 2014, when a snowstorm and avalanches caused by cyclone Hudhud, killed 43 porters and trekkers on or near the pass.

The alarm went off at 3:55am, and when we looked out of the window we could see the stars. We jointly decided to go for it. We dressed quickly, ate porridge by candlelight, and left by torchlight at 5:15am, each wearing nearly all of our warm clothes. Dawn came at 6:30am. By 7:45am we'd passed the highest point we'd reached the previous day. Everything was going well – I wasn't having any problems with my legs, and Sarah was taking slow, deliberate strides and breathing carefully to minimise altitude sickness. Clouds, however, were massing ominously overhead.

Before too much longer, though, Pertemba and the two porters were starting to find the climb hard going, and so was Sarah who was following in my footsteps. Still we pressed onwards and upwards. After very heavy going over snow and rocks, we spotted the summit chorten at midday, and settled down for eggs and chapatis just below the top of the pass to be out of the wind. The clouds were gathering from both sides, so we didn't want to hang around. The good news was that as soon as we started descending, Sarah started to feel better. Against that, crossing some of the traverses in knee-deep snow proved increasingly tiring, the clouds took away the views, the descent seemed endless, and it began to snow in earnest. But we could see a stone shack half a mile away and we sent the porters ahead to get a fire going. It was 3:30pm. We'd been going for ten and a half hours, and we were cold and exhausted.

The roof of the shack had been blown off, leaving only narrowly spaced rafters from which icicles hung down and through which the snow fell. The floor was full of rubbish, and there was no door, though the porters soon got a fire going. Pertemba cooked an incredible meal of soup, rice and omelette. When Valerie and Ron staggered in from the cold, lucky to be alive after being caught in the snowstorm, we shared it with them. They'd hardly brought anything for themselves.

We slept in a tent near the shack's wall for shelter wearing all our clothes – even, in my case, my Goretex jacket – and awoke to find another six inches of snow had fallen overnight. After breakfast, we continued the descent. Not for the first time, I wished I had brought my ice axe from my Tower Ridge climbing days as it wasn't easy keeping my balance on narrow ice-covered paths on steep slopes. At least, though, I had boots. The poor porters had only the plastic bag, string and gym shoe combination already referred to. They deserved better from us, I realised. I felt even guiltier when I realised that they'd made us breakfast and not made any for themselves.

And so down into the once-forbidden valley. Immediately we could see the differences. Whereas the western valleys had lodges with painted names and menus all carefully aimed at passing trekkers, here we were staying with the Nepalese themselves. As I've said, this suited us: there seemed no point in going to the ends of the Earth only to find oneself tied to loud-mouthed westerners. Here were different rules for hospitality, and maybe they wouldn't survive the coming of tourism, but it was good to see all the same. At Manang, Pertemba led us into a house whose owners seemed to be away, but it didn't matter: a neighbour let us in, and Pertemba started cooking a meal in the kitchen. Further down the eastern valley at Pisang, it was a similar story – once again, not a tourist lodge but a home off a side street. In we went, past four cows in the courtyard, up a snowy log ladder to our own room. It amazed us that we could just turn up and were immediately taken in as part of the family to eat the same food and sit around the fire together. There were no formalities, and in one lodge we all shared a bedroom with both the host family, and the porters. Strangers seemed to treat each other as old friends, and the Nepalese hosts were never anything but friendly and relaxed. It was impossible to dislike them.

The valleys were beautiful too. On the southern horizon, the long line of 20,000-footers of the Annapurna Himal marched west along with us: down below, the path through the snow-laden pine forests was easy. It felt, Sarah said, like England. Our young, cheerful porter Pemba, who hadn't been this way before, walked along whooping and singing. A stray dog started following us.

Also following us was Valerie, who came up to us at lunch the next day. We were half-way through our dahl bat – the rather uninspiring Nepalese staple dish of rice and lentils which we seemed to eat a lot more of on the eastern half of the walk – when she breezed in and joined us. We didn't particularly want to spend the next ten days with her and weren't particularly forthcoming when she asked about our plans. We hoped she got the hint. Two days later, she arrived just as Pertemba was dishing out lunch. She helped herself and ignored both him and us.

I'd loved these eastern valleys, but I wondered how long they would remain unspoilt. Already, even though the route was yet to become known as the Annapurna Circuit, its eastern half was beginning to attract tourists: Valerie and Ron, the two Americans we'd met five days into our walk and who warned us of knee-deep snow, the exhausted Japanese man we'd met at Mukintath; and of course, the two of us. Nothing, in fairness, like the numbers of westerners we'd encountered on the first half of the trek, and you could still walk the eastern half of the circuit for two or three days without coming across any tourists. But things were changing already, and even though we were part of that change ourselves, it still felt sad.

Soon, I felt, those houses in which we stayed in the eastern valleys would be just the same as the lodges on the west. They would downplay Nepalese food on their menus and boast about offering lasagne and lattes. The guides and porters would soon know the names of every mountain and village they passed instead of being, as they were now, unable to read maps and being charmingly igno-rant of the name of villages they'd never visited. Children wouldn't shout "namaste"[15] at tourists a hundred yards away nor villagers gather to solemnly inspect them. Although it seemed hard to imag-ine, maybe that easy, effortless Nepali friendliness – so clear that it transcended language – would go too.

Soon, the paths turned tricky as the gorges narrowed and we found ourselves going up and down over loose snowy rocks or endless slippery steps. I found these hard going – in some ways even harder than the Thorong La. Pertemba could tell I was having prob-lems and came back to help, holding onto my wrist which not only

---

15 Namaste – an ancient Sanskrit greeting meaning "I bow to the God within you", usually given as a salutation or valediction and delivered with a slight bow and hands pressed together.

gave me support but meant that I could descend the steps without jarring my spine quite so much.

The Marshyagdi (meaning "raging") river was rushing downhill, and so were we. At Tal – about the furthest point east on the Annapurna Circuit – we saw our first rice field. The villages started to have more livestock in them – chicks, hens, calves. There were more dogs. Bamboo grew in the woods. Houses' bedrooms opened onto the street not the courtyard, as in the northern valleys. Women could sit on their verandahs in the sun and knit, breastfeed, weave and talk. Life was sweet and getting sweeter. For us, though, it felt bittersweet the way the last days of a holiday always do. We were soon about to turn west to Pokhara, and – ultimately – home.

When you read about the Annapurna Circuit, you'll often find it described not as a circuit – the way we walked it, starting and finishing at Pokhara – but as a horseshoe. The start of the walk is given as maybe 20 miles further east of Pokhara, the end maybe 15 miles west (this is, you may notice, doing the walk in the counter-clockwise direction that is safer from an altitude sickness point of view). The roads between the bottom ends of the horseshoe are now so obvious that there no longer seems much point in walking them. Worse – from a trekker's point of view, though not a Nepali's – is the fact that roads now cover the entire route apart from five days from Muktinath to Manang – and each year they edge nearer and nearer to the Thorong La itself.

To Nepalis, the road, is a blessing. Their farm produce reaches market more quickly so their incomes rise. Their access to health care improved so rapidly that within seven years of the coming of the road life expectancy has skyrocketed from 44 to 70. No-one could want to take either of those things away from them. Yet something has been lost all the same.

I said at the start that I would try to explain why walking the Annapurna Circuit meant so much to me, and I can see that so far I haven't done that. For an answer, let me turn back to the pages of Herzog's book, *Annapurna*. Right at the end, when he was trying to sum up what climbing Annapurna meant to him, he wrote the couple of sentences I'm going to quote here. The language is a bit too high-flown for my taste, but there's something in what he says all the same.

"For us, the mountains had been a natural field of activity where, playing on the frontiers of life and death, we had found the freedom for which we were blindly groping and which was as necessary to us as bread. The mountains had bestowed on us their beauties, and we adored them with a child's simplicity and revered them with a monk's veneration of the divine. Annapurna, to which we had gone empty-handed, was a treasure on which we should live the rest of our days. With this realisation we turn the page: a new life begins. There are other Annapurnas in the lives of men."

Having MS was an Annapurna. So was walking the Annapurna Circuit with MS. And as for the beauty of those mountains and those unspoilt valleys – well, perhaps Herzog can say that he saw them at their best. And as for me, I can say that for three weeks as 1980 turned into 1981, I walked the best walk in the world and the best of my life.

oooOOOooo

Chapter 10

The Houseman's Tale

There were 12 of us, one standing at the wall-mounted phone, the other 11 gathered close round him, waiting eagerly. The setting – the mess room of Ipswich Hospital, where I had been working as a senior house officer since February 1982 – was completely nondescript, NHS furnishings never having risen above basic 1970s utilitarianism. But the phone call we were awaiting could hardly have been more important. It was July 1983, and we were hanging around the phone because we were about to find out whether or not we had passed Part II of the MRCP post-graduate medical exam.

If we had, we would be able to put the letters MRCP(UK) after our name. This would tell the world that we were members of the Royal College of Physicians, which likes to boast that it sets a global benchmark of medical excellence. In those pre-email days, the Royal College's method of telling those who had taken the exam whether or not they had succeeded hadn't changed much for centuries. A long list was put up on the noticeboard at its Regent Park headquarters in London. A friend had been given a list of all our names, instructed to go there and to phone us in the Ipswich Hospital mess at an agreed time.

Being an MRCP mattered enormously to every one of us. For those wishing to pursue careers in medicine the exam was essential: in others such as radiology it was desirable, showing a good all-round grasp of clinical medicine. Without it, the specialist career ladder – in my own case as a radiologist, first as a registrar, then senior registrar, then consultant – would be, if not impossible, then probably more difficult. And for the last four and a half years – ever since I had finished my radiology elective in Cambridge in January 1979 – I had not wavered in my ambition. If I started the Eighties coming back from Nepal and the experience of working in an Indian hospital, I wanted to end the decade as a consultant radiologist in Britain.

That was the course I'd set, and I was fully committed to it. Perhaps that was one of the lasting effects of first studying the "wrong" subject at university and then finding myself in the "wrong" job" at Warburgs, the merchant bank. When I finally found the "right" career path, I valued it that much more.

The only problem was that in terms of pass rates, the MRCP exam was the hardest I had ever sat. Or, come to think of it, ever would, because none of the others had anything like an 80 per cent failure rate. I suppose each of the 12 of us at Ipswich Hospital must at times have looked at each other and wondered who would make the grade and who wouldn't, but if so we kept it to ourselves. Although we were all desperate to pass the exam in order to be able to proceed on the specialised medical career paths we had each mapped out, there was no rivalry between us: we genuinely wanted each other to succeed. Gore Vidal, we would have agreed, got it wrong when he said "It is not enough to succeed. Others must fail." Or at best he was only part right: no matter what happened elsewhere, we wanted everyone in our own group at Ipswich to succeed.

The MRCP exam tests knowledge across a vast range of important and common disorders as well as the clinical science behind their treatment. The 18 months I'd spent as a senior house officer at Ipswich Hospital had been ideal preparation. In that time, I had gained experience of four specialties – neurology, chest medicine, gastroenterology and dermatology. My 11 colleagues each had their own similar combinations of expertise and were all on similar rotational posts, which had been purposely designed to give the wide experience of medicine necessary for those medics who wanted to take the MRCP. If we were ever going to pass an exam as difficult as this, we realised, we'd have to pool our knowledge.

That's exactly what we did. Once we'd finished our work for the day, for an hour or two every evening for about eight months we would go back on the wards and examine each other on our own "interesting" patients. Thanks to the reputation of its clinicians, Ipswich Hospital had a wide range of "interesting" cases – essentially, the more unusual ones, which were also the kind on which exam questions tended to focus – and each of us would have come across them on our separate daily rounds. When the 12 of us met on the wards by such a patient's bedside for our early evening study sessions, one of us would know what they were suffering from and the others would hone their diagnostic skills by questioning and examining the patient, just as they would do in a real exam. Examining about half a dozen patients in this way each evening improved our diagnostic skills no end.

I don't know whether MRCP candidates still study like that, but I hope they do. I'd never before experienced this collaborative, mutually supportive, approach to acquiring knowledge, but I found it hugely beneficial. Maybe this collective approach was only possible because we had already bonded by all working the same, frankly ridiculous, hours as junior doctors. In another generation, these would come to be seen as downright dangerous, but the long hours we all put in did at least foster a certain esprit de corps.

Let me give you an example of the kind of hours I'm talking about. Anyone working what we called a "one in two" rota had to work every other night and every other weekend as well as all the days in between. Think about it: every other weekend, you were on call from Friday morning right through until Monday night. All of Friday, Saturday and Sunday nights you mightn't see your bed. In practice, you probably soon learnt how to do without the standard eight hours' sleep and mastered the art of a catnapping.[16]

After a "one in two" rota, a "one in four" was, if not exactly a doddle, then comparatively manageable. Not only did that allow a

---

16 These days, this doesn't happen anymore: the introduction of the European Working Time Directive in 2009 was meant to ensure that all doctors work no more than a 48-hour week. However, as this was at first based on an average across 26 weeks, it didn't make a huge difference. Contracts setting the *maximum* number of working hours per week are more effective: the latest NHS-junior doctors' contract (2016) reduced this figure from 91 to 72 hours per week.

better work/life balance but also allowed more time for study – both my Hammersmith and Ipswich posts were 1:4. And while there is a lot to be said against junior doctors working excessive hours, what sticks in the mind about the three years in which I was working towards my MRCP is the comradeship. We might moan about the hours we had to work – and rightly so – but all the same the very fact that we were all doing them created a sense of teamwork. We were, it genuinely felt, all in it together.

And how, you may ask, did it matter that I had MS and the rest of the 12 didn't? Was there any appreciable difference between us because of it? I tried to make sure that there wasn't. If there is one thing I am emphatic about – and always have been – it is that I never wanted to be treated differently because of my MS. I never wanted to be defined by it, I never wanted anyone to be able to say "Well, Roger's got MS, you know, we'll just have to make allowances." The very thought was anathema to me.

In my climbing days, I used to think that one never really "conquered" a mountain: the mountain had just let one pass. If you took all the care you could, if you were cautious enough and planned everything properly, then you could get by. It's not, I appreciate, an exact parallel, but I felt something similar about MS and my medical training. If I'd had, as a junior doctor, anything like the MS-related problems with my legs I'd had during my pre-clinical and clinical studies at Cambridge, I would never have been able to pass the MRCP exam, let alone anything after it. I hadn't conquered MS, and probably never would, but at least it had let me pass into the medical career on which I had set my heart.

True, sometimes the "arrest" call would sound and because of my MS I wouldn't be able to do anything other than hobble as fast as I could down the hospital corridor towards the sound of a cardiac emergency. But sometimes – months later – the alarm would sound, and I would instinctively respond and find, to my joy, that the MS had let go its grip on my legs and – magically, wonderfully – I could run down those same corridors just as if nothing had ever happened to me.

I mentioned earlier that at Ipswich Hospital I worked in four specialties, each for four months. First up was gastroenterology, which I had also experienced as a house job while at Addenbrooke's Hospital where I had been on one of those "one in two" rotas – from August 1981 to the following January. I followed that by working for a dermatologist, a neurologist and a chest physician. At the end of my attachment to the neurologist, I told him that I had MS. He hadn't even noticed. That was a good moment too.

In my personal life, I must admit, not everything was going smoothly. During my first house job – at Newmarket General Hospital – Sarah and I realised that our marriage had reached the end of the road. It wasn't the fault of the long hours I was working, so much as that we'd just got married too young. I learnt from the experience and moved on, though it was painful at the time. I stayed on at Earl Street in Cambridge and, if anything, threw myself even more completely into my work.

Newmarket Hospital turned out to be a relatively gentle introduction to the junior doctor's life. True, I might still find myself occasionally working a night, a day and a second night without a break, but looking after patients on the male surgical ward – from clerking them in when they arrived for surgery, to making sure all the investigations requested were performed, that blood was cross-matched and so on, to checking that they were comfortable after their operation and finally to looking after them until they were ready to be discharged – all this was a satisfying process, even if somewhat routine. The camaraderie with the other junior doctors was, however, a compensation. So too was the fact that you would have your own bedroom in the hospital, and there was not only a canteen where you could get a meal at whatever time of the day or night you wanted, but a bar in the mess too. It wasn't unknown for a registrar to down a couple of pints there before tackling the afternoon's surgical list. Different days indeed.

Back in the Ipswich mess, while we were all waiting for that telephone call from the Royal College, I thought back to the rest of the three years that had taken me to that point. The six months I'd spent at Addenbrooke's had been more demanding than my time at

Newmarket, but that was only to be expected from a teaching hospital. Against that, I was working for people I knew and respected, the gastroenterologists Graeme Neale and John Hunter. And while I'm not the type of person who is always insisting that things were better in the good old days, for me at least some aspects of hospital life *were* better arranged back then. In those days, clinicians had all their patients together on the same ward, so if you were following the surgeons on their rounds, making sure they had all the information on patients (CT scans, barium studies, etc) you didn't have to dash all over the hospital the way you do now.

My first senior house officer (SHO) post – and my last six-month placement before Ipswich – was at the Hammersmith Hospital. I was very pleased to have obtained this post at what was, after all, the Royal Postgraduate Medical School, with more departments of professorial medicine than anywhere else in the country, and a reputation to match. If I wanted to study at a place that would stand me in good stead when applying for future jobs, Tom Sherwood had told me back when I took the radiology elective two years previously, the Hammersmith was an excellent choice. He was biased, having lectured in radiology there before taking the chair at Cambridge. But he was also correct.

In some ways, plotting a successful career in medicine is rather like plotting a sea voyage: you have to work out exactly where you want to go and how best to get there. Every six months, there were around 12 senior house officer jobs at Hammersmith Hospital, although they were all highly competitive. Few other senior house officer posts had such *éclat*: the renal unit at Guy's Hospital, perhaps, the National Hospital for Neurology and Neurosurgery at Queen Square, the National Heart Hospital at Westmoreland Street were all other excellent London alternatives, but at the time there was more ground-breaking research at the Hammersmith Hospital.

My training there was specialised and demanding but hugely rewarding. To give you an idea of the calibre of the people I was working with, let me tell you about my registrar. In the days when I was a senior house officer (though senior didn't mean much as I didn't have a house officer beneath me and had to do all the work of one), he was just plain Mark Walport, not even a PhD, though he had started work on complement receptors, on which his PhD was subsequently based. So, not yet professor, not yet knighted (2009), not yet the director of the Wellcome Trust for a decade (2003-13), not yet the UK Government's Chief Scientific adviser (2013). At the moment, he is chief executive-designate of UK Research and Innovation: in short, arguably the most important man in British science. The year before I joined, the senior registrar in the department was Carol Black; again, this was long before she became Dame Carol, Principal of Newnham College, Cambridge, second woman president of the Royal College of Physicians, and the person who has done more than anyone else to stop patients dying of scleroderma.

Both of them were working for the man who, in 1982, was my boss too, a mild-mannered, preternaturally young-looking, rheumatologist called Professor Graham Hughes who had set up Europe's first lupus clinic at the Hammersmith Hospital nine years before I started working there. He was already an international expert on lupus (or Systemic Lupus Erythematosus) and had a ward of about 18 or 20 patients suffering from this relatively rare disease and other connective tissue diseases. The following year he described a syndrome, now named Hughes Syndrome, and known colloquially as "sticky blood". This was the cause of the most common, treatable form of repeated miscarriage; once diagnosed, women who might have had as many as a dozen miscarriages, could be treated fairly easily and then have a 90 per cent chance of a normal birth.

Twice a week I'd do a ward round with Hughes, and every day with Walport. Before then, I would have spent up to a couple of hours taking blood from the patients there: the demand was so high just because the hospital was at the apex of clinical research and most such research projects required blood. This was the cutting edge of medicine, where discoveries about "sticky" blood would soon be made, patients' lives changed for the better and lengthened. My part in it all was altogether more basic: conducting routine clinics, standing in for my colleagues on other wards once every four weeks; making sure the clinicians had all the investigative reports they needed; and, of course, obtaining the blood, often from "difficult" vasculitic vessels. (I became, though I hate to boast, rather good at this).

At Ipswich, I left behind the specialised world of connective tissue disorders and immersed myself instead in the kind of things I hadn't seen too much of at the Hammersmith – heart attacks, asthma, diabetes and cancer. All 11 of my colleagues round the phone now had helped me in their way and I hoped I'd helped them in mine.

At the other end of the line, the friend who'd copied down the results from the Royal College of Physicians' noticeboard was starting to read out the list. There was a shriek as one of our female colleagues found out that she'd passed, then tears. A friend I had gone up to Glasgow with to take the exam was told that the news for him was bad and he just sat there, not knowing what to say. "And Roger?" the man at the telephone turned and looked at me and smiled. "It's good news!"

oooOOOooo

Chapter 11

The CT Revolution

I met Sally Stevens on my very first week working as a registrar in the radiology department at Addenbrooke's in September 1983. She was an attractive, intelligent 19-year-old student radiographer from Worcester and had already been in the department for a year when I arrived.

I don't want you to think that scientists aren't a romantic bunch, but the first conversation with her that I can recall was about an exam on the physics of radiography. Sally offered me her physics notes, which I accepted, although having taken an engineering degree I didn't really need them. Still, those notes were a link between us, and one I wanted to make the most of.

A couple of years later we started going out together, although we tried to keep our relationship secret from our colleagues for almost two whole years. Some guessed: my friend Pat Farmer, then working alongside Sally as a radiographer, later told me she decoded what was going on from the looks and glances between us. But for most of our colleagues, it was only in August 1987, when Sally and I announced that we were going off together on holiday to Pakistan, that the penny dropped. By then we were living together and in love and three years later we got married at a quiet registry office ceremony in Cambridge.

Even though Sally and I are now no longer together, our marriage lasted more than two decades and was, for the most part, happy. She always saw past my MS and has been supportive when needed. She has also been a good mother to our children – Elinor, who is now 26, and Owen, who is now 23. Both my children have become central to my life in ways I haven't really expressed so far. Although I wouldn't want to embarrass them, I feel I need to say their importance to me is fundamental and my love for them limitless. Hopefully they know this, so it doesn't matter that I haven't mentioned them that much. Nonetheless, it needs to be said.

Having mentioned the most important people in my own life, I'd now like to tiptoe away from it for a few short pages. Medicine, after all, is more than the story of just one person's life. It is a river of them. And what was going on in radiology – my own part of that flowing river – was nothing less than a scientific revolution.

I don't, you may be relieved to hear, propose to explain the intricacies of the ultrasound features of mucinous biliary papillomatosis or intrahepatic bile duct dilation.[17] Nor do I propose, in just one chapter, to sum up the entire range of radiographic history, achievement, and potential. And don't worry: you won't need to have passed a physics exam, or any other kind, in order to understand it. But I would like to tell you one particular story about a British invention which has radically affected my working life over the last three decades, has altered the way in which medicine is practised throughout the western world and has helped to save millions of lives, although no-one has yet put up a statue to its inventor. Oddly enough, it is a story that also involves the father of my best friend. And the Beatles.

Although I never met him, Godfrey Hounsfield sounds temperamentally rather similar to my father. He too loved walking and climbing, was a workaholic who started his science not at university (he never went) but during the war (as a radar technician). In 1951, he started working for EMI as an electrical engineer and in 1958 developed Britain's first all-transistor computer. His next project – thin film computer memory – failed for commercial reasons, but his bosses kept faith with him and let him choose what he wanted to work on next.

The idea came to Hounsfield – a farmer's son from Newark – in 1967 when he was out on a walk in the country. Suppose, he

17 Although if you *are* interested, I've written papers about both . . .

wondered, you wanted to find out what was inside a picnic basket without opening it: how would you do so? He already knew about radar, so he imagined the process in reverse: instead of sending out beams from a central source to pick out what was on the periphery, why not have the beams converge on a single object – the picnic basket, say – in a series of cross-sectional scans? As the light from the beams attenuates according to what they pass through, and as that attenuation could be measured mathematically, those readings could be digitised and a picture made of a single "slice" of whatever was in the box. Move the basket fractionally and repeat hundreds of times, and you would gradually form a complete picture, or scan, of its contents.

Like many inventions, this embryonic CT scanner could only have been developed at a particular time and place. And this is where the Beatles come in. Since they signed to EMI's Parlophone label in 1961, their record sales had almost doubled the parent company's profits. The project Hounsfield was now working on at EMI's Central Research Laboratories at Hayes in Middlesex – he called it "an Improved form of X-radiography" – was massively expensive, but at least the company could now afford it. Or at least it could with the further help of the British state: Hounsfield's box of tricks aroused enough interest from the Department of Health's radio-logical adviser – oddly enough, given the Beatles connection, another man called Lennon – and the DHSS formed a partnership with EMI, which patented the invention in 1968. Hounsfield was now able to use an X-ray tube and a generator instead of a gamma ray, and this reduced the scanning time from nine days to nine hours. The fastest computer then available took a further two and a half hours to process the results.

Working in secret, Hounsfield and his team experimented on bullocks' and pigs' brains, Hounsfield visiting abattoirs in London and carrying back the brains in boxes to his lab. Once at Hayes & Harlington station, he would walk a couple of hundred yards to his laboratory. Of all the streets in Britain, Blyth Road in Hayes seems to be the one where the nation's creativity was most effectively industrialised: as Hounsfield arrived with his boxed supplies of fresh grey matter, he walked past the factory where all the Beatles' albums (and those of Bowie, Pink Floyd and Queen) went out into the world, marked "Hayes – Middlesex – England."

Even when Hounsfield had become the first person to "see" inside an animal's skull, it still took some time for the radiologist Evan Lennon to find a colleague prepared to try out the new machine on the brain of a living human patient. That happened on 1 October 1971, at Atkinson Morley's Hospital in Wimbledon, and it was a resounding success: "There was a beautiful picture of a circular cyst right in the middle of the frontal lobe," Hounsfield later explained, "and, of course, it excited everyone in the hospital who knew about the project." At the time, I was starting my second year at Cambridge without the faintest idea that sixty miles to the south-west an experiment was taking place that would affect so many lives, my own included.

This triumph of British science and engineering delighted my father. But in the case of the EMI scanner – the "head scanner" as it was known until 1975, when the company produced its first body scanner – he was doubly delighted. For overseeing the whole project was a man called Bob Davies, who was not only one of his own best friends but whose son Peter has been a wonderful and lifelong friend to me too.

Bob and my father had worked together at Metro Vicks in Manchester. They were both apprentices in its research department, although Bob had already graduated from Cambridge. He knew and liked both my parents, accompanied them on their first trips to the Lake District, was a regular visitor to their house at Cheadle Hulme and, later, to the cottage in North Wales. That was where I first met his son Peter. We were both eight, and as we played together, crashing about in the ferns, we hadn't an inkling that one day we would meet again as engineering students at Cambridge, much less share innumerable adventures on board the boat we would jointly own. Neither of us had brothers, but that's what we are and have been to each other.

My father always looked on Bob Davies as a great friend and mentor and followed his career with interest. Among the jobs in management he had already taken, there had been key roles at Hotpoint, AEI, Bowaters and Cambridge Scientific Instruments, where he was managing director. Then, at the peak of his career, he became technical director of EMI Medical. This was at exactly the same time as Hounsfield's scanner – by now known as a computed tomography, CT or CAT scanner – was about to come into production. Its ability to provide clear images of cross-sections of the brain was conclusively demonstrated at the annual general meeting of the British Association of Radiologists in April 1972, and the first three machines were bought by the NHS and sent off to Manchester, Glasgow and the Institute of Neurology in London. They cost £100,000 each (£1.4 million in today's money).

The next three years were the boom years. Hounsfield was building faster and better models and, at the end of 1975, produced the first body scanner. Sales of EMI's scanners were less than £0.5million in the financial year to June 1973, but then they rocketed: £5 million the following year, £20 million the year after that. By 1976, when 17 different scanner manufacturers were competing, EMI still dominated – with 450 out of 650 sold worldwide, and Bob Davies was part of that triumph. Each order came with the promise that the machine would pay for itself within the year. Because of that, EMI could get away with charging a 30 per cent deposit on each machine. Scan times, unconscionably long on the first scanners, dropped away rapidly: 13 minutes in 1975, 1 minute in 1983, 1 second in 2000.

It always saddened both Bob and my father that Britain never held onto its lead in the CT market. EMI moved production to the US, and its hold on the market dissipated as other rivals produced their own machines. By the end of the decade, the CT scanner had just become another one of those inventions that Britain had given the world but let slip through its fingers. But even American historians of science concede that the world owes a debt of gratitude to Britain for the development of the CT scanner, and that it mightn't have happened without a number of concomitant factors:

"It is hard to imagine how the instrument would have gone into production," one is quoted as saying in CA Bartlett's *EMI and the CT*

Scanner "without the support of a company like EMI. The combination of the Beatles' success with the British system of research subsidies and the genius of one engineer broke the cash barrier and changed the face of modern medicine."

These, then, were the trends, inventions and innovations that were amassing in the background as I worked out what aspect of medicine I wanted to specialise in. Three weeks before I started that elective in radiology at Cambridge, on 11 October 1979, Godfrey Hounsfield and the South African scientist Allan Cormack were announced as joint winners of the Nobel Prize for Medicine; indeed Hounsfield gave his Nobel lecture about his CT scanner in Stockholm on 8 December, when I was half-way through my first ever radiology course. In his speech, Hounsfield was already looking ahead to the development of the MRI scanner as the next stage in the radiographic revolution: rightly so, as the first clinically useful full-body human MRI scan was only a matter of months away – a world "first" for Aberdeen Royal Infirmary that happened on 28 August 1980. Meanwhile, "real time" ultrasound machines were being introduced everywhere, and all sorts of other interventionist techniques were being perfected. Whatever form of technology was being used, the human body was being coaxed into revealing its hitherto hidden secrets. And wherever you looked, radiology was leading the way.

For all that, it wasn't the fact that radiology was then so cutting-edge that drew me to it so much as that I could see how central it was to everything else. Not only did what you saw on the scans determine where the surgeon got to work; it also could determine the whole way in which a patient was treated – the "staging" of the disease and treatment that is so familiar to cancer patients. You were seeing more cancers than you had ever seen, but there was now a chance that you could catch them when they were smaller, and before they had spread. Radiology, one of my professors liked to say, was a way of seeing the most interesting patients who came into the hospital – because it would be involved with all of them.

Although I had, in my elective course and in my houseman jobs, seen CT scanners at work and ordered up scans on patients, I now had to find out how these machines – and the others we would use

-- worked. That was at the core of what I was being tested on at the end of my first year as a registrar in the radiology department. Only when I had passed that exam could I move onto the next part of my training as a radiologist, which was both far more practical and interesting: finding out how to use the machines to get to grips with pathology, to study patients with unusual illnesses and abnormal scans. Month by month, the training was becoming more precise, more particular – and, of course, more relevant to the work that we would one day be expected to do as consultants.

There's one thing they always did at Cambridge, and it was a tremendous way of teaching that also bonded the department and gave us an idea of what lay ahead of us. Every morning at eight o'clock, we had a tutorial for an hour. A consultant would take the meeting, there would be about a dozen of us in the room, and we would be quizzed about a set of CT scans or ultrasound results, the questions getting harder and the scans less obvious as you moved up the years.

I loved this diagnostic aspect of the job, collating what we knew about a patient's history with what was up there on the screen, trying to work out the clues about what was really going on within the body. That was part of what I had so enjoyed about those last eight months at Ipswich studying for the MRCP exams, and when he became dean of Cambridge's medical school, Tom Sherwood introduced something similar at Addenbrooke's too. A group of us were chosen as clinical supervisors – it was all voluntary – and allocated a dozen medical students or so, to whom we would be mentors. We would each use all of our contacts throughout the hospital to provide "interesting" patients and then examine the students on them.

I was always quite strong on CT because I had been brilliantly taught. Adrian Dixon, our senior lecturer, was an excellent ideas man, very good at motivating junior colleagues to work on research papers (I worked on four with him), and totally committed to his subject. His intellectual curiosity and charm found their reward in 2008 when he was made Master of Peterhouse, the Cambridge college at which he was made a Fellow more than two decades previously. Back then, he had also been busy leading the fund-raising campaigns for Addenbrooke's to have, first, its own CT scanner, and then its own MRI one.

Cambridge's ultrasound training, however, wasn't quite as good, and because of that in 1988 I applied for and won a competitive scholarship from Kodak that paid for me to spend three months on secondment at the Middlesex Hospital with a man called Bill (WR) Lees who was widely acknowledged to be one of the best ultrasound radiologists in the country. The fact that I wrote three papers with him in those three months shows how inspirational he was.

By then I had been working for two years as a senior registrar in the radiology department at Addenbrooke's, having two years previously passed another exam which entitled me to add a further four consonants after my name. Now, as well as being a Member of the Royal College of Physicians, I also became, in 1986, a Fellow of the Royal College of Radiologists. And when in 1988 I finished the last of those three research papers for Bill Lees, I was finally ready for the job I'd set my heart on nearly a full decade earlier. Whether in ultrasound or CT, I had been trained by the best. I knew I was marketable and was ready to apply for a job as a consultant radiologist. But where?

oooOOOooo

Chapter 12

A Question of Stamina

When I look back at the early Eighties, I can hardly believe how much stamina I still had. MS had a hold of my body, but far from a complete grip: I may have walked with a limp and a stick, but I hardly seemed to get tired at all. In 1983, for example, six years after I developed MS, I went on a ten-day hike in Norway's Jotunheimen mountains. Nowhere else in northern Europe has a greater concentration of mountains more than 2,000m high. It's like Scotland on steroids.

I did that walk – and it would have easily been more than 100 miles – with my friend Jeremy George, a senior registrar at Addenbrooke's. You might reasonably imagine that it was me who had to struggle to keep up, but it wasn't. On the day we found ourselves near the bottom of Glittertind, at 2,464m Norway's second-highest mountain, I went up it by myself and Jeremy stayed behind. The next day – again by myself – I climbed the highest one, Gladhøpiggen, which is just 5 m higher (or 8,100ft all in all). On both days I got up and down so fast that I was back in time for lunch.

Both were easy enough climbs, the sort that a whole family could attempt, and at the height of the summer many families did just that – so many, in fact, that these days hikers often complain about the numbers of people thronging the summit. Not when I was there. I had both mountains to myself, and the views were so spectacular – row upon row of snow-capped mountains and jagged peaks – that the memory sticks in my mind all these years later. At Gladhøpiggen, I could look north, east and south, knowing that there wasn't anywhere higher on the planet for thousands of miles, the nearest higher peak a full thousand miles south-east on the Tatra mountains of Slovakia.

And if you don't find many people with MS walking hundreds of miles across Scandinavian mountain ranges and bagging their Norse super-munros before lunch, you don't find many learning to ski either. Again, this was the early Eighties, again it was with Jeremy George, and again it was only possible because I still had stamina. If MS had left a mark on my health, all those years of mountaineering, hiking, sailing, swimming and competing in modern pentathlon had left a mark on my stamina levels too.

I learnt to ski at a place called Megève, near Chamonix, and after five days of ski school, I could just about manage a blue run. I was never an elegant skier: the MS saw to that. Most obviously, it affects your balance. Your legs are stiffer, not the springy shock absorbers you really need when you ski over a mogul. Because of that, you are less in control; your legs might shake and go into spasm when you are leaning into a turn. In your head, you know exactly what you want to do; you can easily imagine that elegant snowy parabola your skis are about to carve on the slope. Then your legs let you down again, and you're out of control, and gravity is speeding you downhill, so you do the one thing you shouldn't, and lean back and fall. At which point, some seven-year-old French kid will invariably whizz past, making exactly the move you had intended to make, except faster, more cleanly, and without ending up in a crumpled heap.

So no: skiing was never going to mean as much to me as it would do to most others on the piste. It was never going to be the high-octane mix of freedom and adrenalin that they might experience. But I wasn't going to let that stop me. I wasn't going to sulk or feel sorry for myself, because – well, what was the point? All I had to do was to look around me. Even on the nursery slopes of Megève, I could look up and see Mount Rosa, the mountain I climbed with Howard a decade before. I couldn't climb anymore, but at least I was still in the mountains, not in a wheelchair. My legs might be too stiff to speed stylishly downhill, but I could still – just about – sideslip. I couldn't bounce down a mountainside doing eye-catching parallel turns on my haunches, but I would do it in my own way.

The next year, I was back in the Alps with Howard, staying near Verbier in a chalet belonging to a friend's friend. If you know Verbier, you'll know that two of its furthest (four cable-car rides) and most difficult trails are the black runs from Mont Fort and Mont Gelé. And if the view from those Norwegian peaks was spectacular two years previously, the views from both of these were even more so – with a white-ridged panorama including Mount Blanc, the Matterhorn and no fewer than fifty other 4,000m Alpine peaks.

There may well be people who say that someone who could ski as unstylishly and intermittently as me has no business going down a black run beginning at the top of a 3,329m mountain like Mont Fort. I beg to differ. For back then, I had one weapon in my arsenal for tackling the steepest couloir, even if it was one that hardly anyone else deployed there: the kick turn.

It sounds far more stylish than it actually is. In fact, as any skier knows, the kick turn is the one manoeuvre that you can only do when you are stationary. Suppose you're heading towards a piste marker warning that the ground beyond it falls away into thin air: all you need to do is put your weight on the lower ski to bring you to a halt just in front of it. Then you switch direction of your skis, one at a time. The first time you learn how to do it, there seems to be something farcically unnatural about the half-way stage of the manoeuvre, when your feet are next to each other but both facing in opposite directions. Then you lift the other ski to make it follow the first one, and you're off again, this time in the opposite direction. It's the slowest, most ungainly way to zigzag down a mountain, but at least it saw me through the hairiest parts of the Mont Fort black run.

All of this, though, drew deep on my stamina. For each of those downhill kick turns, I had to lift the combined weight of ski and the boot and use my sticks for balance. Once mastered, though, you could use the kick-turn to climb uphill too, for those steeper bits of the slopes when you needed even more traction than you could get from using ski skins in the normal way to climb hills you're then going to ski down. Because yes, there is indeed a way to use even more stamina than what I'd been learning at Megève and Verbier: cross-country ski touring. And I wasn't going to let MS stop me doing that either.

In March 1985, I went on my first ski-touring trip with Howard in the Cairngorms. We stopped to pick up Howard's friend James Jack – who became my friend too – in Edinburgh, and started three days of skiing. The first day at Glenshee, we only managed 470m of climbing, but the next day we climbed 932m and on our last day, when we skied across the plateau from Carn Bàn Mòr to the summit of Sgor Gaoith, we also climbed 828m. I was dead on my feet for the last hour of the final day, but by then we had, after all, been skiing or climbing for at least five and a half hours.

This, though, was only the hors d'oeuvres of my ski touring year. If I could handle a three-day ski tour of the Highlands, Howard reckoned, I might be able to manage ten days' touring across the Austrian Alps in May. Plans were laid at Boat of Garten, where we had all stayed with Mike Geddes and his wife Helen on our trip to the Cairngorms. James couldn't make it, but Mike and Helen decided that they'd come too.

Inwardly, I wondered whether I was up to the challenge. Mike and Howard were excellent skiers: as I have already explained, I most definitely wasn't. Yet being forever last was the last thing I wanted to be: the perpetual back-marker, the one everyone was always waiting for, freezing in the cold as they waited for me to catch up. But what if it was worse even than that? What if, while I could only just about handle three days in Scotland, a tour three times as long and at twice the altitude – and more – turned out to be beyond me? If, on Day 5, the stamina drained out of my legs altogether? If, half-way up some icy Alp, I suddenly developed that old favourite, useless hand syndrome? What precise form would failure then take? The mountain rescue team called out to rescue yet another Brit who had bitten off more than he could chew? A rescue helicopter? The medic explaining to the crew "*Multiple Sklerose. Ja, wirklich!*" Quite apart from letting my friends down, I wouldn't be able to cope with the embarrassment.

Naturally, I kept all such thoughts to myself, both before and after we arrived in Austria. Like the old song says, What's the use of worrying? It never was worthwhile. But if there really was any worrying to be done, we were doing it – unexpressed – for Helen's husband.

Mike Geddes, as I have already mentioned, was one of the finest, hardest British climbers of his generation. He was also seriously ill and having difficulty swallowing his food. He had, the doctor had told him, cancer of the oesophagus.

Being the sort of man he was, Mike wasn't going to give up without a fight. He was going to change his diet. He was only going to eat organic food from now on. This ski-touring trip to the Alps we were going on would boost his health as well as his love of life.

I still think of Mike from time to time, and when I do, it's almost always the same image from our trip to the Silvretta Alps. I see him kicking into the snow up above me. I don't see his face, because it is up against the mountain, just his rucksack on his back as he climbs. And in the rucksack, poking out, some organic leeks, part of his new diet, their dark green leaves gently waving against the sky. I still can't think of a better symbol of hope. And, I suppose, of going on ahead. Because four months later, Mike was dead. He was only 34.

oooOOOooo

The other day, Howard emailed me his notes from our ski-tour to the Silvretta Alps. They contain none of these dark thoughts, no acknowledgement of how illness or death, though still distant, were starting to circle round our small party. Instead, in his customary neat handwriting, with occasional precise maps and line drawings, he carefully records how far we went each day, how high we climbed, how many hours it took us, how many metres we descended, the Alpine flowers we saw, the strength of the wind we felt on our faces. Anyone who wanted to, could use Howard's notes to recreate our journey from hut to hut – Madlener to Wiesbadener to Chamana Tuoi to Silvretta, completing a high-altitude loop on the Austrian-Swiss border – and they would probably be accurate to within a few yards. The currency rates of exchange might be worse now (oh, for the days of 3.145 Swiss francs to the pound!) and the weather might even be better than it was on 4-14 May, 1985, the glaciers might even have slipped back towards the peaks. The natural beauty of that part of the world, however, remains unchanged.

Those notes Howard made prompt a flood of other memories. The weight of our rucksacks, for example: we were not only carrying ropes, crampons and climbing gear, but enough food for a week. The hut – I forget which – that was so deep in snow that we had to enter it through an upstairs window. The easy laughter of friends. The early starts: up at 4:30am if we were moving on, a sluggardly 5am if we weren't. The Silvretta glacier, about a mile wide and apparently crevasse-free, gently sloping, with that mix of soft snow with a harder crust that makes for perfect skiing, even for someone like me.

I started to get the tingling sensation announcing the imminent arrival of useless hand syndrome about halfway through the trip. As it worsened, I could no longer use my ski sticks to balance while making an uphill kick turn, as I needed to do on the increasingly steep valley sides of the Silvretta Pass. I was petrified that I'd drop them and they'd slide away downhill and I'd hold everybody up as I retrieved them. Howard helped out, as unobtrusively as he could, because no-one knows better than him how much I hate MS intruding into these, the best moments of my life.

He took photos as well as making notes. I've got one of them in front of me as I write this. In it, I've strapped my skis onto my rucksack, one on either side. I am working my way up an 80-degree snowy slope. You can't see my face, but it's right up against the snow. You can't see my hands either, although one of them is undoubtedly holding onto an ice-axe which is buried in the snow. Move the picture so that the snow is level instead of almost vertical, and it looks as though I am prostrating myself before the mountain, as Moslems do in worship, bowing their heads so that their nose and forehead touch the ground.

To me, the most wonderful part of the picture is the way in which the mountain falls away behind me. The whiteness of the snow merges with the bluey-whiteness of the sky: there is only the very faintest of lines between the two, so the photo looks almost as if I am climbing up out of the sky. There are black rocks behind me, vertical and unable to hold the snow. They serve, to my mind, as a reminder of gravity, of everything that pulls you down to earth. Though I am faceless in this picture, though its angle looks frighteningly weird, though it's not even completely in focus, I am moving slowly but relentlessly upwards.

I love this photo. Let me tell you why. When I look at Howard's notes, the only time he ever mentions the slopes being so steep that we couldn't skin up them and needed to climb up with our skis strapped to our rucksacks, was on our very last day. We were making our way up from the Silvretta Hut to the Rote Furka Pass. "Strangely," he wrote, "the map suggested that this steep little pass could be ascended on skis – in reality, it's a climb, with skis strapped to the rucksack. The snow is crusty, but occasionally gives way, making the ascent a slow job. The top of the pass is incredibly windswept."

Was this the place at which Howard turned round and took a photo of me struggling upwards with my skis strapped to my rucksack? I like to think it probably was. If so, I almost certainly had useless hand syndrome at the time, because I distinctly remember it coming on halfway through the trip. So I'm climbing, nearly eight years after getting MS, with a wonky arm on top of everything else. The Rote Furka Pass is 2,429m (7,969 ft) above sea level, and according to Howard's meticulous notes, it had already taken us two hours to climb 349m to reach it from the Silvretta Hut in which we had stayed overnight. It would be a further four and a quarter hours before we reached our final destination – the Madlener Hut, where we had stayed on our first night. That I did all of this, and didn't hold back the group despite a schedule that would be physically demanding even for someone without MS – it all seems so gloriously, wonderfully, disease-defyingly improbable, and that's the second reason I love Howard's picture.

Now just suppose I'm wrong about both of those reasons. Suppose its wispy hint of the metaphysical is pure nonsense. Suppose that it wasn't taken at the Rote Furka Pass at the end of our

Alpine ski tour when the useless hand syndrome had definitely set in, but on the first couple of days when it hadn't. Even so, I'd still love that photo. Here's why. Wherever it was taken, to me what it shows is stamina. Even if one hand wasn't working, my two legs were. Affected by MS, certainly. But still capable of carrying me – what was it? Two hours to the top of the pass, plus four and a quarter hours to the Madlener Hut. *Six and a quarter hours*. I had enough stamina in my legs to walk, through snow, in the Alps, despite MS, for six and a quarter hours.

So when I looked at my future on Sunday 12 May, 1985, it was still bright with possibility. I'd got through our Silvretta ski-tour without any problems; in fact, I'd enjoyed it enormously. So we could do it again next year. Mike would get better and he and Helen would come along and Howard and I could go on a ski tour in the spring. In fact, that would be how I would divide up the year: spring for ski-touring, summer for sailing. Why not?

Sadly, it never happened. I owe Mike, Helen and Howard a debt of gratitude for including me on the Silvretta trip, but it only worked because my stamina levels were still so good. They soon started dropping. The more they did, the more that photo came to be a reminder of an unattainable dream. Of all the reasons I've given for loving Howard's photo, this is the most lasting. Like the waving leeks in Mike's backpack, it can stand as a symbol of hope.

oooOOOooo

Chapter 13

Gilgit and Beyond

On the map, it's just over a thousand miles. Fly into Rawalpindi, head north to Abbottabad, and press on to Gilgit and Karimabad on the old Silk Road. Back down the Hunza Valley to Gilgit again, east over the Shandur Pass to Chitral, south to Peshawar and east to Abbottabad and back to Rawalpindi. On Google maps, they reckon that those thousand miles will take you 42 hours non-stop. You could do it all, quite easily apparently, if your car averaged 25 miles an hour.

In 1987, it took us over three weeks, although we weren't in a rush and we weren't in a car either. We weren't in a rush because for years I had been fascinated by this part of northern Pakistan – and not just for the mountains either, though they are every bit as spectacular as you would imagine the meeting place of the Himalayas, the Hindu Kush and the Karakoram ranges to be. But though I'd read up on the Brits who had explored these mountains – Bonington and Tilman among them – for me there was more to it than that too. For places like this were also where the "Great Game" of imperial rivalry between Russia and Britain had been played in the nineteenth century, with an array of compelling characters on both sides, and books about it had filled the shelves back home at Legh Road. Here were the passes across which cannon had been hauled through snow-drifts, where spies in disguise had been hunted down, and where the exoticism of the east met western imperialism in the most spectacular setting possible. No wonder I was hooked; no wonder places like Gilgit and Peshawar hung around in my imagination, usually with the thought "One of these days . . ." loosely attached.

The other reason we weren't in a rush was that these were some of the world's highest and most dangerous roads – often unpaved, narrow, with thousand-foot drops on one side, and reckless drivers coming in the opposite direction.

My ambition of going to northern Pakistan was further spurred on by my 1983 hike in Norway, when I met a couple who told me about the Karakoram Highway and how it had opened up to tourists relatively recently. I bought a Lonely Planet Guide to Pakistan and started dreaming.

Sally and I had been living together in Earl Street since May 1987, and I had interested her in the idea too. Unfortunately, ever since the Silvretta ski tour, my stamina levels had been shrinking; we both knew there was no way I could climb a mountain, nor could I manage a 145-mile hike, as I had done in Nepal. All I could manage at the time was a 15-minute walk. But so what? We could always take the bus.

We flew out on 9 August and arrived at Rawalpindi in the middle of a heatwave. Twenty years later, the airport would be renamed after Benazir Bhutto, who was assassinated in the city; the month after we were there, five people were killed when a bomb exploded at the bus station. Yet our own first impressions were of friendliness: a family we met on the plane kindly dropped us off at the bus station, and the people there could not have been more helpful in pointing out where to get the bus to Abbottabad. Yes, that's right: we knew the place long before Osama bin Laden decided to move in.

Back then, the Pakistani section of the Karakoram Highway started at Abbottabad, winding north for 500 miles to the Chinese border. It largely follows the old Silk Road up through the Himalayas, where it used to be said that you could find your way by the bleached bones of the animals who died there in the winter snow. In the course of its construction, largely with Chinese money and partly with Chinese labour, a thousand labourers died, mainly in landslides in the northern passes, where it is one of the highest paved roads in the world.

Apart from the fact that we were heading north into those mountains, we didn't have any set plans. I remembered Nepal, and how the most enjoyable times had been in the eastern valleys which were still opening up to tourism, not the western valleys which already had. In Pakistan we'd be looking for the equivalent of the former, not the latter: if we wanted to meet Europeans, have corn-flakes for breakfast and sleep in air-conditioned hotels with TVs tuned to CNN, we could have stayed in Europe. Here, though, we were backpackers, free to catch whatever bus we wanted, to go where we pleased, with no aim in mind other than seeing and trying to understand as much of the country as we could.

So, on the Eighth Wonder of the World, as they like to call the Karakoram Highway (a lot more enticing than its official name, the N-35) the 26,660ft peak of Nanga Parbat – the ninth wonder of the world, if mountains are judged by height – lured us north. Below, the Indus swirled south through valleys narrowing to deeper and deeper gorges the further north we went. It never failed to amaze me how the road had been built in the first place, and yet sometimes I could look across the valley and see tracks of even greater improbability, where Jeeps had etched out pathways across 70-degree scree. Whichever side of the valley you were on, it was invariably a long, long way down to the turbulent green glacial waters of the river. Occasionally, you could look down and see the rusting skeletons of lorries on the rocks in the chasm below, *momenti mori* lingering uneasily in the mind as the bus swayed ever further onwards.

Gilgit was a bit of a disappointment, but the Hunza Valley wasn't. Back then, parts of the road were still unmetalled, but the valley seemed a place apart: indeed, for most of its history it seems to have been. Only in the last 150 years has it opened up to the rest of the world. My guidebook described it as "the Shangri-la of the Karakorams", and it's easy to see why: this is a valley in which the mountains rear up higher and more dramatically than most Europeans will ever have seen. Yet the valley floor is green, flat and fertile, dotted with cypresses, fragrant with orchards and bright with flowers. Apricots were always grown here – indeed, I could buy Hunza apricots at my local shop in Cambridge – and you would see them drying on the house rooftops, even if the cloud of insects feasting on them would put you off. The Aga Khan, spiritual leader of the Ismaili Shias who lived in the valley, had persuaded farmers to grow cherries and peaches along with their usual cash crops of wheat and potatoes.

He has done a lot more. Thanks to the backing of the Aga Khan's charity, this part of Pakistan is free of the poverty, pollution, religious extremism and poor schooling (especially for women) that are so evident elsewhere. The Ismaili Shias believe in female equality, so women have better educational opportunities and health facilities than elsewhere in the country. We toured a medical centre in Karimabad and were impressed by its excellent child vaccination and follow-up programme. And the more enlightened education policies didn't just result in 95 per cent literacy rates for girls (in many parts of the country these are merely 5 per cent). Attitudes to women are different too. On our travels elsewhere in Pakistan, men would stare at Sally, as she walked along, carrying her rucksack: it was almost as if they couldn't understand the very idea of female independence. Here, they did. Shangri-la indeed.

Sadly, it's a Shangri-la that most westerners will never see. After 9/11, bookings to hotels so relatively near Afghanistan fell away completely. The 2013 massacre by Taliban militants of ten climbers and their local cook at the base camp of Nanga Parbat was a further block on tourism. Even without the threat of external terrorism, sectarian tensions ran deep. Less than a year after we visited Gilgit, for example, hundreds died there in anti-Shia riots.

At Gilgit, we met a man who worked out an itinerary for us that would show us the unmissable sights of the Hunza Valley. He recommended a hotel in Karimabad (the Silver Jubilee Hotel, now no longer in business) that was run by a nephew. When we got there, he in turn introduced us to his cousin, Jon Sakim, a trek organiser. Jon had – or claimed to have – impressive credentials. Not only had he been to the summit of Nanga Parbat with the legendary Austrian climber Kurt Diemberger on his 1981 expedition with British climber Julie Tullis, but he had been on the disastrous British K2 expedition in 1986 in which Tullis and Alan Rouse both died. "You a friend of Rouse?" he said, in one of those "small world" moments. I nodded. "Me a friend of Alan Rouse too!" he exclaimed.

The Hunza Valley is, British explorer Eric Shipton once wrote, "the ultimate manifestation of mountain grandeur . . . the most spectacular country I have ever seen", and Jon volunteered to take us wherever we wanted. How about the Nanga Parbat base camp, he suggested, or the one at Rakaposhi, or maybe even going across the Shandur Pass to Chitral? Where did we want to go? Rakaposhi was the nearest. It's a huge mountain – over 12 miles long from east to west, one of the few on the planet to have an 18,000ft sheer drop from the summit to its base – and its snowy bulk completely dominated the view across the valley from our hotel. Sally tried taking a picture of it in the moonlight from our hotel window. It didn't turn out, but I can still see it in my mind's eye.

We decided we'd try a less strenuous expedition: my legs had been bad, and I didn't want to overface myself. Jon had mentioned a short walk to the nearby Ultar glacier. We could all camp in a meadow he knew by a shepherd's hut. There were spectacular views and – best of all, during a heatwave – the glacial stream would quench our thirst.

We set off at 7:30am, carrying the tent and everything we'd need for an overnight stay. Soon it became so hot that Sally waded into one of the glacial pools fully clothed. She was completely dry just 15 minutes later. We climbed a bit more, then rested for a while in a meadow by the stream, splashing each other with water and soaking our clothes to keep cool. Then onwards and upwards to the shepherd's hut, which we reached at 4pm.

Jon insisted on putting up the tent, although for some inexplicable reason he pitched it among a pile of sheep droppings. He also commandeered the stove, but made a hash of lighting that too. He went off to sleep in the shepherd's hut and we went to bed early.

During the night, I developed a high temperature. Whenever this happens, my legs are always badly affected. That was happening right now. I could no longer walk, and whenever I tried to do so – as when, in the middle of the night, I got out of the tent and tried to walk away to urinate, I kept falling over – taking one particularly nasty tumble over a small ledge. Sally gave me lots of Aspirins and lots of water to drink, but we had stupidly forgotten to pack the Steritabs and as the stream water came from near the sheep pens, we were probably only making things worse.

Probably? Certainly, more like. Because in the morning I was so weak that I could hardly stand. Jon carried my rucksack and led the way back down to Karimabad, but after about an hour I realised that I just couldn't carry on. I couldn't even stand up.

We decided that the best thing to do was for Sally and Jon to press on back to Karimabad and get help. I'd stay where I was, halfway up the valley, just above the meadow where we had relaxed the previous afternoon. I found some shade next to a large boulder and waited, shivering.

Two and a half hours later, Jon reappeared with a friend, and they started to carry me down across the moraine. We were still about 2,500ft above Karimabad and the path was frighteningly steep. It was appallingly hot and dusty, and I was so weak that I could barely hang on.

Finally, we made it to the valley floor. There, Jon explained, I'd have to walk, as they didn't want to carry me ("Not good for women to see man being carried"). Propped up between them, I staggered the last three-quarters of a mile back to the hotel. I was running a temperature – the following day I was still 102.5°F – and had severe diarrhoea. I just wanted to sleep and sleep. No sooner had Sally put me to bed than she became ill herself. And that was us on Friday 14 August 1987, Pakistan's independence day, exactly 40 years since it came into existence. Outside, in Karimabad, as everywhere else in the country, there were firework displays, patriotic songs, and processions in which everyone dressed in the national colours of green and white. Inside, in the Silver Jubilee Hotel, two exhausted Brits slept on.

We slept all the next day too, and resurfaced on Sunday. We'd met a nice German couple who wanted to get across to Chitral and we agreed to hire a Jeep between us. With, it's important to add, a driver too. On these roads, that was a necessity – unless, that is, you feel competent about jump-starting a Jeep with a faulty ignition by driving in reverse on a narrow track with a gorge on one side. That happened to us at one point, and I'm certainly glad I wasn't at the wheel at the time. Being a passenger was scary enough.

The Shandur pass on the road from Gilgit was probably the most spectacular of the ones we went across, and the least busy too. It stays that way most of the year, except in July, when a polo festival is held between teams from Gilgit and Chitral on an incongruously perfect ground at the top of the pass – at 12,139ft the highest polo ground in the world.

The best moments in any holiday, though, usually aren't when you see the sights on the tourist trail. These might be impressive enough – the vaguely Tibetan-looking Baltit fort at Karimabad, for example, is every bit as imposing as Edinburgh Castle itself – but even better are those times when you get a real sense of what life really is like in a country.

These usually happen completely by accident. I'll give you an example. On the way to the wild, narrow, and impossibly high hair-pins of the Shandur Pass, our driver saw a man sitting beside the road. We were in the middle of nowhere, and I don't know how on earth he knew we were coming, or how long he had waited for us. But he knew our driver, who slowed down and talked to him. He invited us into his house, served us tea from an amazingly elegant China tea service, produced the most delicious apples we'd had since we'd arrived in Pakistan and invited us to have lunch. First, he indicated, he'd have to catch it.

Sally fell asleep for an hour and was woken by a baby's cry. A group of women were looking at her as if they had never seen a western woman before (which was entirely possible). The baby belonged to a woman who looked about 15 but who turned out to be the man's wife. The baby was wearing a heavily-beaded cap and masses of dotted blue-grey make-up round her enormous brown eyes. When the baby cried, she breastfed it, when it wet itself, she wiped it with a rag which she then rinsed out and washed the baby's bottom with water from a pool. The man came back with six brown trout and prepared a simple lunch of chapatis and spinach and crisp, fried, fresh trout. And that's all it was, no more and no less. Just a perfect lunch with perfect strangers.

Sometimes, though, those encounters last in the memory not because of any mutual comprehension but because of its opposite. Again, a quick example. The nearest we got to the Afghan border was the Kalash Valley. To be allowed access, we had to obtain a permit at the Deputy Commissioner's office, which involved stepping back in time to an office whose furniture had remained unchanged since the Raj and having a cup of chai. The Kalash people of Pakistan's North-West Frontier Province, my guidebook told me, were pagans who "live in windowless mudstone huts and use neither soap nor money."

These people, the guidebook should have added, are the last surviving Kafirs of Kafiristan. If you recall Rudyard Kipling's *The Man Who Would be King*, or if you've seen the 1975 film starring Sean Connery and Michael Caine, this was the land in which two European adventurers became revered as gods. The novel contained a few slivers of truth. Kafiristan was a real place, its people – now cleared out of Afghanistan and surviving in small numbers (less than 4,000) in the Kalash valleys – are indeed Kafirs, or pagans (well, polytheistic, certainly not Muslims), and they do indeed have more European features – including fair hair – than people who live in the surrounding areas. Because of this, it has often been surmised that they were descendants of the army of Alexander the Great: indeed, in Kipling's novel, this is why the two rogue British soldiers seem plausible rulers to the Kafirs.

The Greek connection with the Kalash probably isn't true, but the Kafiristan one is. Yet the future the Kalash face was already uncertain even 40 years ago when our Jeep nosed up the atrocious roads into their valleys. Already, the war in Afghanistan against the USSR-backed regime had forced thousands of refugees to flee across the border into Pakistan: we passed some of their camps – houses that were little more than piles of stone with heavy-duty canvas tents for roofs. There were hundreds of children, and although most waved, some shook their fists. At the time – long before 9/11, long before US drone strikes – we wondered why.

These days, the Kalash face problems on all sides. Afghans routinely make incursions into their lands and rustle the few cattle and goats they possess. Militant Islam is potentially an even deadlier threat. If that doesn't get them, western culture (mobile phones, fashions), deforestation, education, better roads bringing more non-Kalash settlers who use money instead of bartering, and the corruption of tribal leaders who sell off their hand-crafted icons, probably will.

We'd planned to stay, but didn't. The local hotel was dirty, we couldn't find the spring that was supposedly the only source of hepatitis-free water in the village (we'd both only just recovered from Karimabad) and we headed back to Chitral instead. Before we left, I took a few photos. In one of them a young mother looks straight back into the lens with an unconcern I had hardly seen anywhere else in Pakistan. Her young son – fair-haired – sat next to her, looking back a bit more quizzically, but still with the air of someone who is used to being photographed. The men, I noted, sat around with the children and played and talked to them. I hadn't seen much of that in Pakistan.

The Kalash woman was beautiful, black-haired and open-faced like a young Martine McCutcheon. She was wearing a black cotton long dress brightly embroidered around the hem, shoulders and cuffs with red, yellow and white stitching in a pattern that seemed to be echoed in what her young son was wearing. But I couldn't imagine what the future would hold for her in that remote valley any more than she could imagine the world I was about to go back to.

From Chitral, we took the bus to Peshawar over the Loweri pass – an appalling road, with the usual spectacular gorges, to which we were now becoming inured. Although the bus called itself the Afghan Express, it crawled up to the top of the pass in five hours at little more than walking pace, finally only pulling into Peshawar at 10pm, a full fourteen and a half hours after we had set out from Chitral. As you can imagine, we were exhausted.

We gave ourselves two nights to recover and completed the rough quadrilateral of our journey by taking the bus from Peshawar to Abbottabad. As Peshawar is so near to the Khyber Pass – and hence Afghanistan – it was widely thought to be a staging post through which US-funded arms found their way to the mujahideen fighting the Soviets. They in turn were blamed for the bomb attacks on local banks, government offices and – most worryingly from our point of view – bus stations, their own version of the "great game" perhaps, but one that differed markedly from the 19th century version that had long intrigued me. On the day we finally left Peshawar, I got on board our bus and waited impatiently for it to start. Sally had noticed an empty briefcase by the ticket office, and had become – understandably – worried by it, although she only mentioned this after we had left. We pulled into another bus station and waited for another 20 minutes. This time I was worried too, and by the time we pulled out, the sweat was pouring off me, and for once it wasn't just the heat.

Security checks were reassuringly thorough at the airport – so thorough that they even took my stick away to be re-examined before we were allowed to board. Forty minutes from London, Sally nudged me. "Mont Blanc down below," she said. I stood up to look out of the window. It was indeed. We must have already passed the Silvretta Pass, but there beneath us was a perfect bird's eye view of Mont Blanc, the Mer de Glace, Chamonix, Les Aiguilles and the Midi-Plan Traverse which Howard and I climbed back in 1973.

Whether there or in Nepal, whether in the hills above Karimabad or the valleys of the Kalash, I thought to myself, at least I have seen more of the wonders of this world than most, multiple sclerosis notwithstanding.

oooOOOooo

Me ski-mountaineering in the Silvretta Alps. (1985)

The road from Gilgit to Chitral, in Pakistan's north-west Frontier Province. (1987)

Fort at Karimabad in Pakistan's beautiful Hunza Valley. (1987)

*A Kalesh woman and her fair-haired son. The Kalash are thought by some
to be descendants of Alexander the Great's soldiers. (1987)*

Lochs Coruisk and Scavaig have always been special to me. Here I am on my first visit with Diana and my mother, during our family cruise on Zuleika. (1967)

Stac Lee, Stac an Armin and Boreray (from left to right). (2014)

Loch Scavaig, Loch Coruisk and, towering above both, the Cuillin Ridge.(2015)

Sailing with Peter on the West Coast of Scotland. (2015)

'Liberty' – our trusted vessel for ten years' of island sailing. (2014)

Me helming Martha Maria, en route to the Lofotens. (2011)

Midnight, Arctic Norway. (2011)

'Pelagic Australis', north of Disco Island, Greenland. (2009)

West Coast of Greenland. (2009)

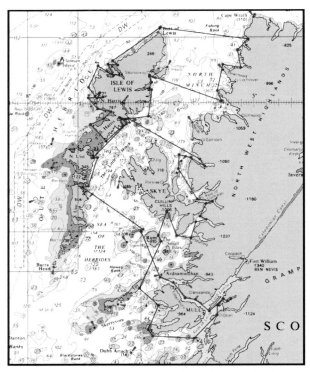

A typical summer cruise wandering through the Hebrides. (2014)

Friends for life: me, Howard Steen and Peter Davies in Oban. (2014)

Chapter 14

Salford Royal

For a short while, I thought I'd begin my career as a consultant in Chesterfield. The hospital there had a lot going for it, and on a personal level it made sense too. First of all, it was only an hour away from my parents' house at Prestbury; secondly, the road there ran through the Peak District. I might not be able to climb its rock faces any more, but it would still be good to live within sight of its moors.

Then, in the pages of the *British Medical Journal*, I saw that Hope Hospital in Salford was looking for a consultant radiologist specialising in ultrasound. The work I had done with Bill Lees would, I realised, make me a strong candidate for the job. Plus, of course, Salford was a key part of our family's story, and Prestbury wasn't too far away from there either. So I went to both hospitals for an informal chat about the jobs.

At Hope Hospital, I was shown around by Hari Mamtora, who had been head of radiology at the linked Salford Royal Hospital.[18] My first impression was not favourable. The single CT scanner they had – and which was used for patients from all over the North-west of England – was almost antediluvian, and walking around the hospital's seemingly endless corridors tired me out. What I was really looking for was a hospital that was altogether more forward-looking, better equipped and – for the sake of my legs – more

---

18 The two subsequently merged after Salford Royal was closed.

compact.[19] By the time I got back to Cambridge, I had made up my mind. I wouldn't bother applying for the post at Salford.

That night, I had a phone call from Hari. He knew I hadn't been sold on the hospital, but wanted to persuade me to change my mind. The whole place, he said, had tremendous potential, not just the department but the hospital too. That old CT scanner would soon be a thing of the past; as a future head of the radiology department, he would push hard to make it a centre of excellence, with equipment to match. His hopes for Hope Hospital were infectious: by the time I put the phone down, I had decided not to withdraw my application after all.

Over the next three decades, during which he became a good friend as well as a trusted colleague, Hari Mamtora's optimistic predictions turned out to be true, not least because of his own hard work and dedication. Salford Royal NHS Foundation Trust, to give it its current title, is different in so many ways from Hope Hospital, its predecessor on the site. For one thing, it's now about five times larger, with no fewer than 7,000 staff, is one of only three in England rated as "outstanding" by the Care Quality Commission and also as the best in the whole country in respect of its use of digital technology. Instead of the one antique EMI CT scanner – which was literally taken away to be a museum piece five years after I arrived – it now has four, along with four MRI scanners, all of which work round the clock, providing images to be interpreted by 28 consultant radiologists as opposed to the six who made up the department when I first arrived.

One issue about the job was that Salford wished me to cover obstetric ultrasound – about which I only had a rudimentary knowledge – as well as general ultrasound. Adrian Dixon, then a senior lecturer and one of my Cambridge mentors, suggested a possible solution. A friend of his who was chairman of the University of Maryland Hospital Department of Radiology had asked him if he

19 As I found out when I worked there, the University of Maryland Hospital in Baltimore is a great example of a properly planned hospital: Helicopter pad on the roof, A&E and radiology on successive floors directly beneath and everything else in the hospital radiating out from them. Quite right: radiology should be central!

knew of any radiologists who would like to go there to teach general ultrasound techniques. I could certainly do that, and in the process pick up all I needed to know about obstetrics ultrasound. Provided Salford agreed, I could even go to Baltimore with the title of visiting assistant professor for a six-month sabbatical. Thanks to pressure from Hari Mamtora, Salford did agree, and so from October 1988 to April 1989, that's where I went. Sally had a job there too: building on her work as a radiographer in the MRI unit at Addenbrooke's, she held a similar post in Baltimore.

I have already mentioned the scientific revolution that was unfolding through the increasing sophistication of CT scanners. Something similar was happening with ultrasound, the capabilities of which vastly improved during my 30 years as a consultant. The obstetrics work in which, thanks to my six months in Baltimore, I now had some expertise, could sometimes prove very stressful, especially when I had to scan obstetric anomalies picked up by the sonographers. But at least I could now provide reliable advice to those mothers worried about foetal problems; I was also asked to write the chapter on these in David Sutton's standard textbook on radiology, and later rewrote it in three successive editions.

On the other hand, there were times when working with diagnostic ultrasound was hugely enjoyable. To some extent, other technologies separate radiologists from their patients. I could always have a brief, reassuring word with a patient whose CT scans warranted it and who had questions about the process, and wherever possible, I did that. But with ultrasound, it was easy enough to talk to the patient while examining them: indeed, it would probably feel odd to them if I didn't.

When I started at Salford, each week I had three lists of general ultrasound patients, with up to a dozen people on each list. On each list, there was always someone whose experience of life I'd find memorable. Over the years, that adds up to far too many to recall, but I do remember one patient telling me about being torpedoed twice while serving on Atlantic convoys during the Second World War and another telling me about being in Singapore and helping emaciated Allied prisoners of war board his ship after being released from Japanese POW camps. Others would tell me about their work helping troubled teenagers on Outward Bound-type weekends, or the simple joys or running their local football teams. I always marvelled at the sheer number of patients who engage in voluntary activities to help others – those "little, nameless, unremembered acts of kindness and of love" in Wordsworth's phrase. They never make the headlines and it may indeed be easy to forget about them, but if there is one thing my ultrasound patients made me remember each week, it was that there are a lot of good people out there.

Not only was I in an excellent teaching hospital, but I was in a job that, over the years, increasingly played to my own strengths. Ever since my time at Addenbrooke's, training with Chris Flower, I had picked up his passion for chest radiology. When I joined Salford, there was no committed chest radiologist, although one consultant, who was soon to retire, had a minor interest in the subject. I made sure that the chest physicians knew how keen I was to specialise, and when that consultant retired, I made a bid to replace her and do more work as a chest radiologist. This was enthusiastically accepted, and I instituted a dedicated clinical radiological meeting every Friday afternoon with the chest physicians. This continued, with almost no interruptions, for the remainder of my career.

When I began at Salford, there was only one CT scanner for an 800-bed hospital and its use had to be carefully rationed to the cases that would most clearly benefit. But Hari Mamtora soon worked his promised magic: more and better scanners were installed, and more consultants were employed. Although in those Friday meetings with the chest physicians we must have discussed thousands of cases, there was not a single one which subsequently turned out to be a misdiagnosis or result in an adverse incident or patient complaint. That fact alone is testimony to the calibre and ability of my colleagues – Anna Walsham, Anna Sharman and Fran Hampson among them – and is a true cause for pride.

At Salford, we wanted to go even beyond that. It has long been known in many hospitals that some radiology reports describing possible lung cancer were not acted upon. This could happen for a variety of reasons: before computers, radiology reports might disappear in the internal mail, or be sent to the wrong person. But even when the report reached the right person, they might read the main report about why the X ray was done but not notice that vital extra paragraph further down describing a subtle, unexpected finding (or, if a non-specialist, not understand its significance). My colleague – and good friend – respiratory consultant Ronan O'Driscoll recalled a particular case from the late 1990s that served as an example of what we were trying to prevent. A patient had been admitted with a heart attack, and the clinical team thought the chest X-ray was clear. A radiologist subsequently identified a possible small lesion in one lung and advised a further follow-up chest X-ray and a CT scan to check if the lesion was still visible. Sadly, the report was filed away in the notes with no action taken. The patient presented with lung cancer two years later.

Ronan, Peter Turkington (also a respiratory consultant), chest consultant Simon Taggart and I devised a system to ensure this never happened again. Any radiologist reporting an unexpected lesion would flag it up in a "safety net" system which required the radiology secretaries to alert the consultant in charge of the case and highlight the fact that there had been an unexpected finding. The lung cancer team would then check after a few weeks to ensure that action had been taken.

Simple and obvious? In theory yes, but in practice I had to ensure that every radiologist in the department changed their working practice. Yet soon the benefits were clear. Subsequent audits showed that, in our hospital alone, about two cases a month of lung cancer were diagnosed more quickly as a result. The safety net system soon spread from being lung cancer-specific to a hospital-wide service. After a presentation to the British Thoracic Society in 2005, the "Salford safety net", as it became called, was taken up by many other hospitals. In 2008, Salford Royal won the NHS patient safety award; thanks to implementing the safety net, we were officially the safest hospital in the country. Ronan reckons it wouldn't have happened without me; I think he's wrong, but I won't protest too much.

oooOOOooo

It's an odd thing, trying to sum up my life as a consultant. Many professionals might feel the same. You attain your goals, you take the job you'd set your heart on, you learn to live with its responsibilities. You do your best to train, encourage, set standards and ensure they are kept. You keep that skill-set – knowledge, observation, training, conscientiousness – so sharp that you'll never miss those tiny shadows that might turn out to be tumours. And then what? The best part of three decades flash by, the way they didn't all those years when you were starting out and wondering whether you'd pass those first exams, then the ones after them, and so on. Looking back, I can see that each of those stages in my career were just that: they led on to somewhere else, they were easy to remember, easy to describe. When I became a consultant, by contrast, my ambition had plateaued: there was no further step I wanted to take.

I was clinical director of the department from 1998-2005, which involved looking after a large budget (£12 million in 2007) and bidding for medical equipment against other departments and hospitals. I think I handled the pressures of the job well enough, but much of that was down to the support of the highly competent radiology business manager and his or her team. But my heart was never in admin, and the powers that went with the post were tightly circumscribed: just how tightly I realised when I mildly queried one employee's travel expenses and was immediately threatened with a British Medical Association tribunal at the very least. After seven years, I felt I'd done my bit for the department and was relieved to step down from the post: just being a consultant radiologist with great colleagues in a great hospital was job satisfaction enough for me.

And how did I manage with MS in a hospital I almost turned down because I couldn't manage the distances? Even when Salford Royal was still called Hope Hospital and was correspondingly smaller, it was still 350 yards from one end of the department to the other, and in the new hospital those distances were even greater. What that meant was that each day I would plan ahead. I would work out where I needed to be at what particular time, and if that took me to the other end of the hospital, I would make sure that I could take care of anything else that needed doing while I was there.

Throughout my years as a consultant, I worked hard at maintaining my stamina by keeping as fit and active as I could. Most days, I cycled the 15-minute journey to and from work, and on Saturdays I would swim 80 lengths (a mile) in the pool. When, aged 62, I took partial retirement and reduced my working week from five to four days, I also swam a mile on each of my Monday and Friday half days. Needless to say, I never smoked: as a chest radiologist, I saw the consequences of smoking every day of the week.

I had no serious relapses of my MS in the 28 years I worked as a consultant, although I had several minor episodes which dragged on for months, making walking a bit harder and occasionally causing problems with my hands. None of this, however, interfered with my ability to do my job, and I never took a day off due to illness in all that time.

The one exception to this is that for the last 15 years I have had to use intermittent catheterisation to empty my bladder. This is one thing that, although I wasn't wheelchair-bound, links me to most of those who are – or at least those with spinal cord lesions. Like them, I had to do this up to six times a day, and like them, this introduced a risk of urinary tract infection, for which it was necessary to take continuous prophylactic antibiotics. Every six months or so, I'd get a breakthrough infection, occasionally requiring intravenous Gentamicin infusions. Because I was so implacably determined that my MS wouldn't affect my work, I would plan things so I could receive the infusions as an outpatient in the emergency admissions unit at lunchtime. I did the same thing when it came to having my six-monthly cystoscopy to paralyse my bladder muscle with botox. In both cases, when I got off the couch and told the nurses that I was going straight back to work, they thought I was being stoical or stupid or both, but really it was just a matter of getting the most out of life.

If I didn't love my job, maybe I would have lingered a little longer in the recovery room of the outpatient theatre department. But there were always new scans to report, always new notes to dictate, more patients to discuss, diagnoses to make and colleagues to brief. In any case, my department was in another building across the car park; I'd better hop off the bed and get walking.

oooOOOooo

Chapter 15

Worse than MS?

The Nineties started well. We were four months into owning a beautiful six-bedroomed Victorian house overlooking a parkland golf course five miles northwest of Manchester and a 15-minute bicycle ride from my work. We were busy turning it into a home. Our daughter Elinor was born in April 1991. We gave her the middle name Rona after the Hebridean island on which I had proposed to Sally. Three years later, our son Owen was born.

New life, new home, a job I loved and a wife I loved too. By the time Elinor was three, our life had fallen into the daily routine of full-tilt new parenthood, tiring but fundamentally content. I would usually get back from work at about six o'clock, help to make the meal while Sally fed Owen, and we would take it in turns to bathe Elinor and read her a bedtime story.

MS might have taken away some of the joys of life, but these new ones – reading the happy-ever-after stories to my three-year-old daughter in the soft light of her bedroom, watching my son fall asleep in the cot next to us – remained unaffected by it. Until suddenly, and tragically, and in the one moment I would give anything to change, they were.

I was driving home from work at about 5:30pm on 1 June 1994, when I killed a woman.

I wasn't speeding, but just doing marginally over 20 miles an hour on a road I know well and was about half a mile from home. Normally I cycled to and from work and can't even remember why I was driving.

A double decker bus had stopped at a bus stop, and the car in front indicated that it was going to overtake. There was another car coming in the other direction but I thought there was plenty of time for us both to overtake the bus.

I then realised that the car in front wasn't going to overtake at all but had braked and stopped. I tried to brake too but the car didn't slow down.

I don't know whether my foot hit the accelerator instead or just slipped off the brake. All I know was that I couldn't use my legs to control the car. In that split second, it seemed to me that I had three options. I could carry on and overtake, in which case I would hit the oncoming car, as it was by now much too near. I could keep straight on and hit the car in front, making it crash into the bus. Or I could swerve to the left, mount the pavement and hit the wall behind it.

I couldn't see anybody on the pavement, so that's what I did. Except instead of hitting the wall, I found myself driving along the pavement. And the pavement, as it turned out, wasn't empty at all. There were two people on it who had just got off the bus. The first, an 82-year-old woman, went under the car and died as a result of her injuries. The second, a man, went over the car and suffered no major injury.

I was totally mortified and in massive shock. My whole career as a doctor was all about saving life and yet now, as I found out later that evening, I was responsible for somebody's death.

This, to me, was far worse even than having multiple sclerosis itself. The whole day became a nightmare, and one that refused to go away. When I attended the police station the next day, the police claimed that I had been deliberately trying to undertake the bus on the inside (to get home two minutes early?) and I was charged with manslaughter. Although this was later reduced to causing death by dangerous driving, the police claimed throughout that I had always been fully in control of my vehicle.

Until my own dying day, I will never lose the feeling of shame that I have caused the death of another human being and am still distressed by the suffering I caused to that poor lady's friends and family. I have relived that day time and again, forever trying to work out what I could have done differently, or what it was about that one day I could have changed. Maybe it was the rain: the soles of my shoes would have been wet, and maybe that was why they slid off the foot pedals. Perhaps, but I'd never noticed that before. Maybe, and more likely, my legs were tired by the amount of walking I'd done that day between the various departments in the hospital. Perhaps, and certainly my legs were generally clumsier the more tired I got, but I had never before noticed it affecting my driving. Maybe it was because I'd had flu for the previous couple of days, because I had slept poorly the previous night, and looked so sick that clinical director of the department had advised me to take the day off. And true enough, as I had noted in Karimabad in 1987, a high temperature does indeed take a toll on my legs.

Hindsight, though, is always 20:20. I'd never taken a day off work because of my MS, and had dosed myself with aspirin to keep my temperature down. I had patients booked that only I could deal with. As for only having had two hours sleep, I'd survived on less as a junior doctor. We all had.

The question you are probably asking yourself is what on earth someone with MS was doing driving a car in the first place. The answer to that is my driving licence was and is conditional on passing a medical every three years. I had always done so, the last occasion being two and a half years before the accident.

If the doctor who examined me then – not my own GP, but someone appointed by the DVLA – had done any more than a cursory job, the accident might never have happened. A proper examination would have shown that my MS had progressed to the stage at which I needed a car with hand controls – the kind I have driven, entirely safely, ever since.

The other big "if only" concerned the law. If only the Crown Prosecution Service had taken any notice of two expert reports who both pointed out that my MS had left me with impaired sensation in my right leg and that this probably caused the accident, justice could have been done a lot sooner.

In the end, after two horrendous years, it was. The case was thrown out at Bolton Crown Court on 30 April 1996, when the police accident investigator admitted that the prosecution's version of events could not possibly have happened. Neither I, nor any of the defence witnesses were even called into the witness box. Behind closed doors, it was agreed that the charge of dangerous driving would be dropped if I pleaded guilty to a charge of careless driving. On my lawyer's advice, I did so, to avoid the unpredictability of a jury verdict. I was fined £200, had seven points added onto my licence, and the defence costs were returned to me. At the end of the case, even the judge admitted time had been needlessly wasted. With two or three witnesses and some medical evidence, he said, the real cause of the accident could have been established a year earlier.

As it was, for the best part of two years, I lived under the shadow of suspicion. Everyone who had ever been in a car with me knew that I was a careful driver, not the kind of person who becomes enraged by other drivers, or who takes reckless chances. When, a few years later, I took an advanced driving test, it was no surprise to anyone that I passed with top marks in every single one of the 30 different categories. I am naturally cautious behind the wheel of a car, just as I am when skippering a yacht or just as I used to be while climbing a mountain. Speed doesn't interest me – if it did I'd have probably bought something other than the lowest-powered Ford Orion on the market. Drugs (never) and drink (never when driving) don't interest me either. I am, in fact, almost pathologically law-abiding.

Until those charges against me were finally thrown out, though, I lived with the possibility that I could be sent to jail for being something I am not. If I had been sent to prison, my career would have been over. I would be the killer doctor who deliberately – *deliberately!* – had tried to undertake a bus by driving on the pavement. We'd have to pay £60,000 in legal fees, and Sally and the children would probably have had to move in with my parents. As I descended into a pit of depression, I started wondering what prison would be like.

And then, at 1am on 3 September 1995, while I was still in the middle of the legal nightmare about causing death by dangerous driving, another body blow.

The phone rang, and I picked it up to hear my father. "Roger, it's Alec. We've had an accident. Mum's dead."

He was ringing from a hospital in Warsaw, where someone had wheeled him to the front desk and the only international phone they had. He was still in pain, having fractured his sternum, collarbone and several ribs in a car crash just hours earlier. That, though, was as nothing compared to the loss of my mother, the love of his life.

My father had been giving a paper on human factors in manufacturing at a conference and they were spending their final two days with their hosts at their country cottage outside Warsaw.

They sat in the back of the car as their Polish friends drove them back to the city after an al fresco lunch in the sunshine. A car overtaking a bus hit them head-on. My mother was killed outright.

I was devastated. We all were. My mother had always been a tremendous support in everything I'd ever done. Even in the court case, hers was always the face I'd turn to from the dock, to see her half-smiling in encouragement and shared incomprehension at the legal nightmare pursuing me, first through two magistrates' court appearances, and then on to the Crown Court.

In December 1995, she wasn't there, but my father and sister were in her place. This time, our defence team had everything ready; all our expert witnesses had turned up from all parts of the country. Unbelievably, the prosecution hadn't notified their civilian witnesses to attend, so the whole case had to be put back again for another five months. The agonising wait for what I hoped was justice continued. Only on 30 April 1996 was that cloud finally lifted.

Throughout, I continued to keep working. At work, I kept myself to myself and only my closest friends would have had the faintest idea what I was going through. Those same friends would probably also tell you that I tend to keep my emotions on a tight rein.

That's almost the only way in which I can begin to talk about my sister Di, who took her own life on 23 May 1998. She has flitted in and out of these pages, and I know that I have failed to do justice to her. She is worth a book in her own right, one that would also show another Chisholm who also loved the mountains and climbing, who also went to Cambridge and became a doctor because she wanted to do some good in the world. She did too: first as a psychiatric registrar, then as consultant and finally director of public health for Manchester, she did tremendous work for the underprivileged and minority groups in the inner city.

I can't presume to know how mental illness took hold of her towards the end of her life, although I know that she, too, was floored by our mother's death. I also know the high regard in which she was held by so many people from all walks of life. When she died, my father received over 200 letters of sympathy from senders ranging from mountaineering friends to a government minister, from the lady who cleaned her house to her health service superiors. Across the board, the same qualities were mentioned: she was kind, she inspired love, and she fought the corner of people in need. Her death may have ended her own inner torment, but it left a huge gap in the lives of those of us left behind.

oooOOOooo

Chapter 16

Gale Force

I can still remember the first time I ate lobster, even though it's 47 years ago. We were in a hotel restaurant in Harwich, there were four of us round the table, and we had all ordered the lobster – not in its shell but with a delicious creamy cheese sauce – as a starter. And the reason I remember wasn't anything to do with the meal, but because it was practically the first thing we had eaten for three days and we all felt fortunate to be alive.

It was September 1970, just a week or two before I went up to Cambridge. Hugh, a fellow-apprentice at Rolls-Royce, had asked me to help bring his father's boat, a long-keeled Harmony 31 (a slightly smaller but similarly seaworthy version of the well-proven Nicholson 32 design) back to England from the Baltic. There were four of us: Hugh, his father, myself, and another of his friends. Hugh's friend and father were both badly seasick and confined to their bunks for three solid days of a particularly stormy crossing.

The expedition started easily enough. We got to the boat by ferry to Rotterdam, then hired a car to Kiel-Holtenau, at the Baltic end of the Kiel Canal, where she had been left at the Joint Services' Yacht Club. We picked her up and, for a small fee, hitched a lift from a passing barge for the 61 miles through the canal. Sailing was not allowed on the canal, and the under-powered petrol engine mightn't have managed. But the engine wasn't really the problem. The weather was.

By the time we reached Brunsbüttel, the German port where the Kiel canal meets the north shore of the Elbe before it flows into the North Sea, the shipping forecast was reporting gale-force winds not only in German Bight – where we were – but in practically all other sea areas. An intense low-pressure weather system had settled over the North Sea and showed no sign of shifting. We waited for two or three days in Cuxhaven. When the forecast finally indicated that the winds were moderating in our sea area, we set sail – to a rousing chorus of *Rule Britannia* from the crew of a neighbouring British yacht also summoning up the courage to make the same voyage.

The Elbe estuary is a dangerous place at the best of times, with a tide that runs at 4 knots on the ebb across the Scharhörn Riff sandbanks on one side, and one of the world's busiest sea lanes (all the shipping to and from Hamburg) on the other. We were just making our way out into the wider reaches of the estuary at night when the gale came back with a bang. It was a north-westerly, right on the nose of the boat. We had to beat into it for three whole days.

I had never been out at sea in a gale before, and nor had any of the others. Forty-seven years later – in every one of which I have sailed as often as I could – it remains the only gale in which I have ever been trapped. I've read about them, of course: at Legh Road, our shelves were full of books about adventures at sea, of storms, gales and even hurricanes survived. Every one of those writers would mention the wind shrieking through the rigging, and that's exactly how it was. Not just blowing, or blowing as hard as you can imagine, but screaming. Screaming at you like you've got no right at all to be where you are, out on a boat at night, on a lee shore 200 miles from home, on an estuary even more dangerous than the open sea. And the sea itself was raging too, with waves even higher than the mast of the boat. How many times had I read about such things? When I did, I'd try and fail to imagine it. Waves higher than *Zuleika's* mast, as we sailed up the Minch three years before on the first boat my father chartered for a family holiday? Waves as high as the masts of *Lady Loo* or *Morning Flame*, two yachts in which I had crossed the Irish Sea in the previous year?

I could almost imagine it, but there was always something missing: an edge of controlled panic, a casual realisation that one might not survive. Another thing about actually being in a gale that I had never picked up from the books I'd read was that the scream of the wind wasn't constant. It varied: loudest when you were at the top of the wave, then almost absent in the trough, the next immense wall of water providing brief shelter. The saving graces were that the waves were regular and not breaking, and that the Harmony was a long-keeled, seaworthy design that rode the waves almost like a cork. There was the occasional crash if she fell off the back of a wave but, as we became attuned to the conditions, those occasions – which could do damage – became fewer.

Early on, Hugh had managed to reduce the sail to the minimum combination of storm jib and trisail. We ploughed on into the night. All the time we were on a lee shore which, as all sailors know, is when the wind is driving you towards the shore so that you'll be wrecked if you don't battle against it. Hugh's father and his other friend were both hopelessly seasick down below, so it was up to Hugh and me to keep going. In the darkness, we could just make out the loom of the Texel lighthouse on the horizon. We couldn't yet see the lighthouse, but we knew that survival depended on being able to steer a course towards its weather (windward) side. Anything else, and we would soon be wrecked on sandy, low-lying land.

The lighthouse got nearer, the light at first just a distant glow, the darkness gradually brightening, over the next 12 hours, to an actual beam. Hugh and I slept turn and turn about for three or four hours at a time, steering away from the lee shore and battling north-west – still in the gale, but now merely crossing one of the world's busiest shipping lanes –towards England. On the evening of the third day, with the sea completely flat and the wind calm, we motored into Harwich. For the last five miles we even towed a larger boat that had suffered engine failure. And so, hopelessly tired and dreadfully hungry, to lobster starters, a lavish main course, and bed. Bliss.

It didn't put me off sailing. I was already irredeemably hooked. I had been ever since I first mastered the basic arts in *Ayeesha*, our family's dinghy, on Redesmere, an artificial lake six miles from home to which I used to cycle, with the sails in a large rucksack on my back. *Ayeesha* came with us on family holidays to Scotland, where we would take it in turns to sail her or paddle in a two-man folding canoe, which we also brought along.

On the sheltered sea-lochs of Scotland's west coast, I learnt some of the basics of sailing. I added to that knowledge over three successive August fortnights at the Menai Straits Regatta in North Wales with school friends Robert and Paul, as well as occasional outings on cousin Richard's self-built plywood dinghy Cadet on Llyn Padarn. As I mastered the skill of balancing the boat between wind and water, I felt the thrill of the boat responding and skimming across the water. I also learnt the basics about tides and how, out at sea, I wasn't the most important thing in the world but comparatively insignificant, and easily endangered by a sudden change in wind or tide.

At Brentwood, meanwhile, I read practically everything the public library had on its shelves about boats. Joshua Slocum's 1900 classic *Sailing Alone Around the World* – in 1899 he'd been the first person to do it – might seem a bit dated now, but the 15-year-old me would have agreed with Arthur Ransome's assessment: "Boys who do not like this book ought to be drowned." Eric Hiscock's *Around the World in Wanderer III*, which was written in the mid-1950s, was another book that left a mark, with its then revolutionary idea that an ordinary couple could contentedly sail round the world in their own boat. I was also reading everything I could find about ocean racing: while other boys my age were drawing E-type Jags or Spitfires, I would spend hours drawing diagrams of what my ideal yacht would look like from the outside and its best possible interior lay-out. Back home, my parents deliberately didn't have a television set in the house, but cunningly packed the front room shelves with books about sailing as well as mountaineering adventures. It worked.

They also fed my sailing addiction with almost every family holiday we had. In 1967, when I was 15, my father chartered *Zuleika*, a 36-foot Bermudan sloop, for a fortnight. We picked her up at Tobermory and headed north around Skye, stopping off at (of course) Loch Scavaig, and reaching South Rona before heading back via Mallaig. This, it seemed to me, was the best life possible. Eric Hiscock himself – by then I'd read his books about short cruises around the British Isles as well – probably had ordered his own life along similar lines. His *Wanderer II*, on which he sailed from England to Scotland and Ireland, probably wasn't too different.

Two years later, on *Lady Loo*, another yacht chartered for a family sailing holiday, we sailed to Ireland. Back then, there was no GPS, and once you were out of sight of land, unless the boat had a Decca navigational system or you had complete confidence in your own ability at dead reckoning (plotting your course and using the ship's log and tidal data to work out approximately where you were) it was easy to get lost. This almost happened to us on our first Irish Sea crossing. We had been out of sight of land for hours and were bobbing around somewhere between Holyhead and Dun Laoghaire, when my mother got one of the frights of her life. My father was lying on the cabin floor and he didn't appear to be moving. He was feeling sick and exhausted by the effort of trying to work out our position. Somehow, he revived, and navigated us safely into Dun Laoghaire. Once we had safely moored, my mother served up the most reviving stew I've ever eaten. And that was another early lesson: that when you're sailing, life has an intensity and is never boring. There will be extremes – lost, with a collapsed skipper on a lumpy sea; in a safe berth, laughing about it all later – but there will never be boredom. There's one positive side-effect of this: you can go for a weekend's sailing, and return feeling as though you've been away for a whole week.

I could give you hundreds of examples of that, especially after 1997 when I had my own yacht, but from the earlier years, one will suffice. And for that, I need to introduce you to Bob Bradfield.

These days, Bob is retired, and spends weeks on end pursuing his hobby. As this is for hydrographic surveying and cartography, and as he concentrates on the anchorages and channels off the West Coast of Scotland, it's fair to say that few people know that part of the world better.[20]

I first got to know Bob at Cambridge, where he was studying engineering at St John's in the same year as me. We didn't spend too

---

20 Bob's unofficial large-scale electronic charts ("information created by yachtsmen for yachtsmen") can be found on www.antarescharts.co.uk. We always use them!

much time together – while I was off climbing, he was often away sailing – although we did subsequently keep in touch when working in London, where he was starting on what turned out to be a glittering career in the City while I was starting what turned out to be its opposite at Warburgs. One July evening in 1976, he 'phoned me at our house in Balham. "Roger," he said, "I have just acquired a nice little 31-ft wooden sloop. Do you fancy coming sailing sometime?"

The wooden sloop was *Inigo*, which he kept at Portsmouth. Sarah and I, Bob and a friend of his called Mandy had originally planned to sail across to France, but before we drove down from London, he told us that we wouldn't be able to do so. There had been problems with the engine's alternator, which hadn't been repaired in time. Instead, we'd have to content ourselves pottering along the Solent and maybe along the coast to Poole or Swanage. We arrived at Portsmouth at 9 o'clock, loaded up all of the food and drink we'd need, and switched on the radio for the shipping forecast. Southwesterlies were promised for the whole weekend, and it seemed a shame to waste them. We changed our plans. Engine or no engine, we decided, we'd sail to France.

In the dark, we glided downriver, into Portsmouth harbour's masses of lights, frigates, floating cranes, submarines, and ferries, and then back into the empty dark of the open sea and out towards Cherbourg. After six hours gilling about off Nab Tower and the Isle of Wight we eventually anchored in the outer harbour (anything else was impossible without an engine). The next morning, we sailed to Omonville-la-Rogue, 11 miles to the west, arriving early on Saturday afternoon, beating into the harbour despite strong tides, rocks and reefs. The sun was shining: this was, after all, the fabled summer of '76. After anchoring safely, a landing party rowed ashore and loaded up with plenty of vin rouge, baguettes, peaches and apricots. The forecast continued to promise south-south-westerlies varying between Force 3 and 5, which would be ideal for a fast sail back home. We'd have plenty of time, we reckoned.

At midnight on Saturday night, though, the wind dropped away altogether. The sea was like a mirror. Except it wasn't. Underneath that calm surface, a tide was pulling us at 3-4 knots towards the Alderney Race.

To all my landlubber friends, I need to explain about the Alderney Race. It's nothing to do with horses, cars or athletics. Think of the coast of northern France. From Calais to Brittany, it generally falls away in a south-westerly direction as the English Channel widens. The one exception is the Cotentin peninsula thrusting north towards the south coast of England. Cherbourg is the main port at the top of the peninsula and Cap de la Hague is its most north-westerly promontory. Eight miles of sea separate Cap de la Hague from Alderney, the most northerly of the Channel Islands. Those eight miles are the Alderney Race, a treacherous strait of enormous potential tidal power – so great, in fact, that the French are planning to use it to generate electricity. At their worst, equinoctial tides can run at up to 12 knots. The tide already pulling us west was nowhere near that magnitude, but soon it would be pulling us south, ever further away from England and from all possibility of starting work on time on Monday morning. With the continuing absence of wind, the sails hung uselessly above us.

We prepared for the worst. It would, we decided, be better to be swept south and out of control down the Alderney Race on the French (or east) side of Alderney, rather than on the island's west side, where there were rocks everywhere. We thought about inflating the dinghy just in case, but it seemed prematurely melodramatic. But we did everything else we could – we even tried using the dinghy's paddles in a desperate attempt to stop being pulled into the Race. Needless to say, it didn't work. I went to bed prepared to wake up to bad news, or worse.

All these years later, I can still remember waking up a couple of hours later and hearing the gurgle of seawater along the planks of the boat. I knew what that meant. A little north-easterly breeze had sprung up while I had been asleep and was taking us out of the danger zone. France started to fade into the horizon by 7:30 on a blue-skied sunny Sunday morning and we were heading home at a steady 5 knots in a Force 4. By 4:30pm we were passing the Needles lighthouse, and by 9 o'clock we were back in Portsmouth harbour and finally ghosted up to a buoy in the dark which Bob managed to grab before we swept past. And that was us. Three days, two foreign ports, a lot of calm – and, above all, no engine! We were back in London by 2am and at work by 9am. Had that little breeze not arrived when it did, though, instead of being at our desks in the City, the Alderney Race would have driven us south and we would still have been somewhere on the north Brittany coast. And that would have taken a little explaining . . .

Sarah and I had one more epic sail with Bob almost exactly a year later, this time not for a weekend but 12 days. We sailed, again in *Inigo*, from Falmouth and made slow passage (all of three days) across the Irish Sea to Baltimore in West Cork. As one would expect, the *creac* was mighty, and we had great times in Ballydehob, Berehaven and Sneem. The highlight, though, was a night passage from Schull that took us to Skellig Michael, one of the extraordinary stacks rising well over 600 feet straight out of the sea off the Kerry coast. We took it in turns to climb the steps to the summit, where the monks lived on what clearly must have felt like the very edge of the world. I've never yet met anyone who has managed to land on those islands from a yacht, and these days, apart from a limited number of licensed tours, it is prohibited altogether.

Two months after we got back, I fell while running down the steps after seeing my course director at St John's, and my life changed for ever. The subsequent MS diagnosis meant that I couldn't climb any more mountains. But it certainly wasn't going to stop me sailing.

oooOOOooo

Chapter 17

Passage to Village Bay

Sailing has always meant so much to me. After MS, it meant even more. If I could no longer climb the mountains I wanted, at least I could sail the seas. Sailing meant I could still test myself against the elements, and provided me with the measured risk, camaraderie and sense of achievement that climbing had always done.

Above and beyond all that, though, is the sheer joy of being out on the water, and seeing light sparkling on the sea, in all its myriad moods. There is nothing that beats that feeling you get when the sails slowly fill and the boat leans gently with the wind and you hear the gurgling of water under the hull, and see the bow wave ahead and the stern wave spinning out astern. Then the boat starts to take off effortlessly. It's a magical feeling, and one I cannot have enough of.

In 1991, I worked out that, so far in my life, I had spent 211 days and 34 nights at sea and had sailed 6,988 miles. Those numbers will have soared since I bought a boat of my own. By now, in terms of days at sea, I've probably racked up almost two full years. I only wish it could be more.

I worked out those numbers back in 1991 not out of nerdishness but because part of my RYA exam for Offshore Yachtmaster required me to document my experience. That 400-mile trip through a gale from Kiel to Harwich I mentioned in the last chapter was a valuable addition to that list, as was the engine-less and worryingly becalmed weekend trip to Normandy with Bob. So were many memorable voyages I haven't mentioned, like a fast passage across a North Sea

lit up by truly spectacular sheet lightning in July 1985[21] or the fortnight's voyage I skippered in a chartered yacht in June 1988 from
Dunstaffnage to Plockton in which I not only proposed to Sally but
introduced my friend Howard to the joys of sailing.

And then, on Wednesday 10 May 1990, when Sally and I were on
Sentosa, a Dehler 36, on a fortnight's holiday as paying crew, there
was the moment I first saw St Kilda.

There are more books written about St Kilda than any island of
its size in the world, and when you sail there, it's easy to see why.
First and foremost, there is the difficulty of getting there. "Don't
bother," a Harris fisherman warned me in 2001. "It's much too far
out. Stay as close to the coast as possible." Unless you have a
decent enough weather window to contemplate a 40-mile dash
out into the Atlantic and back, that's sound enough advice. But
the lure of St Kilda has been so strong that I have sailed there on
three occasions.

The first time was the easiest. The weather was perfect, and we
sailed around the stacks close to Boreray before landing on Hirta.
Boreray is easily Scotland's most dramatic island – a black volcanic
rock thrusting 1260ft straight out of the ocean. "Had it been a land
of demons," wrote yachtsman RA Smith, who sailed there in 1878,
"it could not have appeared more dreadful." Yet the sea stacks
around it – Stac an Armin (at 643ft, the highest monolith in Britain)
to the north and Stac Lee to the west are no less impressive. Anyone
who, like me, has ever climbed sea cliffs can only look on them
longingly, but I could see that merely starting the climbs would be
dangerous enough: at the best landing point on Stac Lee, the Atlantic
swell moved the boat up and down by five metres or more.

The next day, at six minutes to midnight, we landed in Village Bay
on Hirta, the main island of St Kilda's tiny archipelago. It was from
Village Bay that the last remaining islanders were evacuated 60 years

---

21 This was when I was crewing for one of the senior doctors in Ipswich on what was
meant to be a trip to the Frisian Islands following the route Erskine Childers gave *Dulcibella*
in his 1903 thriller *The Riddle of the Sands*. In a long-keeled yacht with a 6ft draught, this
turned out to be a bit of a non-starter but was good experience all the same.

before we arrived, and it was there that everyone who visited the island anchored too, from the islands' Mesolithic settlers to the 100 redcoats looking for Bonnie Prince Charlie in 1746, to Anthony Trollope on a sightseeing tour in 1879, to the German U-boat commander in May 1918 who fired 74 shells at the island's radio mast before departing. (The mast remained standing, some houses were damaged, and one lamb was killed).

When we rowed ashore the next morning, we were met by a young Army officer, complete with swagger stick under his arm, who commanded the detachment operating the island's missile tracking base, which consisted of a huddle of unsightly green-painted concrete buildings by the pier. The Army manned the base until 1998, and didn't mind serving a pint or two to passing yachts-men at the Puff Inn, which they ran and claimed was the most remote pub in Europe. Now the base is privatised, this no longer happens: the public are no longer served, and only people working full-time on the island (contractors and National Trust staff) are allowed in.

It was to be another 11 years before I returned to St Kilda. This time, though, it was in my own boat. I bought *Minella*, a long-keeled Van de Stadt-designed Trintella 29, from my cousin Mike. She was launched in 1969, and her first owner was a man after my own heart – Arthur Birtwhistle, a pioneering British cliff climber who later developed a passion for sailing, and who had already sailed *Minella* to St Kilda. *Minella* was a slim boat, with limited accommodation by modern standards, but seaworthy and reasonably swift despite her waterline length of only 21 feet.

To me, there are proper boats and what I call "plastic fantastics", lightweight boats that may skim across the water but can't be depended upon in heavy seas. *Minella* – like all the boats I have owned and nearly all the ones I have sailed in – was a heavy-displace-ment boat with a well-designed hull that meant she could ride over quite steep and breaking waves. She was a boat that went well, whether into or off the wind, a boat that would look after you, that you could rely on to claw you off a lee shore. You could trust her with your life, and we did.

So that's how I remember her, on my second trip to St Kilda in 2001, picking her way through the Atlantic swell on our way to the islands, yet with only a gentle rolling and pitching motion down below as I plotted the course at the chart table. That was the other important difference from my first visit: this time, I was the skipper. And while responsibility, I've always found, may concentrate the mind, it also concentrates one's enjoyment in achievement.

Sally was away in Australia with the children for a few weeks, visiting old friends. For two weeks in July 2001, I was sailing to St Kilda and beyond with two of mine: Dave Conibear, a dentist who lived just across the golf course from me, and Hugh Burnett, a Manchester gastrointestinal radiologist and colleague at Salford. In those years, Dave was the most regular of my shipmates on *Minella*, and as well as loving sailing every bit as much as me, he was totally trustworthy and great company. Together we sailed her on innumerable weekends, sometimes round Anglesey, often to Porth Wen or Port Dinllaen. He also accompanied me on four return trips from North Wales to the Hebrides, of which our St Kilda trip was just one.

Like everyone who knew him, I was devastated when Dave died in 2004, but when his wife Helen asked me to give the eulogy, I had so many golden memories of the good times we shared on *Minella* that the only problem was which ones to leave out. There were so many unforgettable moments just from that trip we made to St Kilda three years earlier. The dozen dolphins that accompanied us, playing in and out of the bow wave as we sped north through the Sound of Islay. The lone fisherman on Loch Mariveg, halfway up Lewis, who stopped his boat alongside *Minella* and, without saying anything, tossed a couple of lobsters into our cockpit before joining us in a dram of Laphroaig. Lazing beneath blue skies and a hot sun in the fields beside the Quoile River off Strangford Loch in Northern Ireland. Battering down the Irish Sea back to Holyhead with a north-westerly moderate Force 4 breeze filling the spinnaker as we surged past the Mountains of Mourne on the starboard quarter and the Isle of Man to port.

But St Kilda itself was easily the highlight. We had reached the islands in just four and a half days from *Minella*'s berth at Port

Dinorwic in the Menai Straits. We had spent the previous night on Barra, at the foot of the Outer Hebrides. The morning shipping forecast made clear that we would have three days before strong winds, possibly gale force, would arrive. A three-day weather window: just what you need if you want to attempt to reach St Kilda out in the Atlantic and get back safely. We decided to go for it. At eight o'clock that evening, it was Dave who first spotted the islands. They were straight ahead, he shouted down to me in the cabin. "They can't be," I replied, remembering the last time 11 years ago, when the summits first appeared above the clouds when we were only four miles off. Now we were 19 miles away. But when I scrambled up the companionway, I saw that he was right.

Through the crystal-clear air, the distant jagged teeth of Hirta rose up on the northern horizon. As we sailed on into the evening, we were treated to an extraordinarily beautiful landfall. A layer of black cloud hung close overhead, as the sun set in the west behind the stacks the moon emerged on the port bow, and Boreray grew ever larger to starboard.

We sailed round to Village Bay, and dropped anchor just after midnight. The next morning, I peered over the side of the boat at a pattern of ripples which I assumed was a reflection from the clouds. Not at all: it was the sandy bottom, seen through 18 feet of water. There did indeed seem to be something pure about the place. This was, for example, the year of the foot and mouth epidemic, and one condition of us landing had been that we would launder clothing to 50°C and keep it in sealed bags until landfall, then wash our shoes in a large foot bath of detergent. Fair enough: foot and mouth ravaged the rest of Britain, with innumerable funeral pyres of animal carcasses. But St Kilda remained uninfected, and held wonderful memories for all of us.

I sold Minella to Dave the following year and bought another boat, a Rival 34 called *Eugie*. But although she was a seaworthy boat – she crossed the Atlantic three times with previous owners – for some reason I never really took to her. After three years, I sold her and, along with two friends – my oldest friend, Peter Davies, and

Steve Henderson, a Manchester GP([22]) – we jointly purchased *Liberty*, a Rival 36, which had already amply proved her seaworthiness by taking her previous owner round the world. She has been a wonderful purchase, handles very well, has looked after us for over ten years and has given us many hours of great happiness.

On Sunday 29 July 2012, as the London Olympics were getting underway, Pete, our good friend Tim Jeans, and I boarded *Liberty* at Oban and set off north up the coast we know and love so well. After the first week, Tim had to go back to London (he had tickets for some of the Olympic events), so we dropped him off in Ullapool and headed across the Minch to Scalpay, on the south-east coast of Harris.

When I was trying to explain why sailing means so much to me, I forgot one important reason. To me, it's so obvious that I wouldn't even think about spelling it out. To a non-sailor, I now realise, it might not be.

It's this: that a sailing holiday is, I think, the ultimate expression of freedom. You can go – literally – wherever the wind blows. In a sailors' paradise like the west coast of Scotland, whatever direction the wind takes you, there is, almost inevitably, a scenic anchorage, an island to explore or some sheltered coast on which you can find a mooring. But at the same time, that gift of freedom comes accompanied by responsibility. Wherever you go, you have to make your way back. You also have to notice everything: the wind, and what it might do, the sea, and the way the tides will move you, the charts, and the rocks that might lie beneath the surface. So freedom – yes, but a freedom whose limits you have, all the time, to work out for yourself.

As an example of what I mean, take that night Pete and I anchored at Scalpay. We could indeed go anywhere the wind blows, but we had given ourselves two choices. First, we could carry on down the east coast of the Western Isles, past Rodel, with its magnificent old church, a reminder of the island's half-forgotten Catholic heritage, and on to Lochmaddy. We could then venture further south, perhaps

22 Tragically, Steve died aged only 55 of a rare and aggressive form of cancer.

mooring near Eriskay, that small but perfectly formed Hebridean island that was not only the real-life setting for the *Whisky Galore!* story but also where Bonnie Prince Charlie landed to launch the 1745 Jacobite rebellion. And on, perhaps to Barra, where we had spent the last night before heading off to St Kilda back in 2001. All of that would be wonderful.

Alternatively, we could turn west through the Sound of Harris and sail to St Kilda.

At one o'clock in the afternoon, we still hadn't made up our minds. Then the shipping forecast came on and told us that there'd be north-north-easterlies blowing at Force 4 or 5 for the next 48 hours. We'd go, we decided, where the wind took us. In this case, 15-20 knots of wind on the beam for virtually the whole 40-mile crossing to St Kilda.

We were just through the Sound of Harris and still a long way from St Kilda at eight o'clock that evening when I noticed that the tiller didn't seem to be working properly. There was a yellow buoy and a rope trailing from the stern of the boat, presumably a lobster pot wrapped around the rudder. Clearly this would slow us down and might dangerously reduce our ability to control the boat.

If you don't sail, you might not think this is a big deal. Inconvenient, yes. Pete or I would just have to jump overboard with a pair of giant cutters and, as darkness fell, somehow sort it all out. Except at sea, there are rules about what to do on occasions like this. And the first rule is: call the lifeboat and/or the coastguard. The nearest lifeboat station is at Barra, and they do wonderful work, but the prospect of waiting for them to make the 40-mile journey up to cut us free made our hearts sink, just as it might have made theirs. And this, I suppose, means that I really ought to add a caveat to what I said just now about the unlimited freedom of a sailing holiday. Sometimes, just as in life, you're not as free as you really want to be.

This time, though, we were lucky. Somehow, by gybing to port, we detached ourselves from the entangling rope. Free again, we carried on sailing towards St Kilda. Pete stuck on a Rolling Stones CD and turned up the volume. A pod of dolphins appeared, ducking and diving under the bow as we sailed, relieved and elated, towards St Kilda. Magical moments like that become memories that stay in the mind forever.

We sailed once more into Village Bay and dropped anchor in calmer waters, 100 yards or so from the jetty, at 2:50am.

We woke at 9:30am, 90 minutes before the first of the tourist boats arrived from Leverburgh on Harris, and disgorged its passengers (who had each paid £195 for the trip). We too, of course, were tourists, marvelling at the same things tourists to St Kilda always had: the unique fauna (the Soay sheep and the long-tailed mice, twice the size of their mainland counterparts), the spectacular setting, the islanders' diet of seabirds, and their vanished Gaelic culture. Underlying all of that, though, was something else, something I had felt at Skellig Michael all those years ago: a sense of being right at the edge of the known world.

The only difference between us and the tourists piling back on board their cruiser at four o'clock was that they knew that they were returning to Leverburgh. And Peter and I . . . well, this is where we're right back to the freedom of sailing again. We would sail overnight, we decided – but which way? West to Harris south-south-west to Barra? In the end, we decided to sail south of Barra to Mingulay, another island abandoned by its inhabitants (in 1912, even before the St Kildoans left in 1930). That very freedom of choice and freedom from schedules is, for me, a key part of the lure of sailing. So too are the discoveries that you make en route, which seem that bit more special because you have chosen the route yourself.

Take that very day as an example. After an overnight passage, the next morning we were motor sailing past Sandray – another abandoned island (1934) – when we saw a sandy bay that, especially on a cloudless day like this, looked positively Caribbean. We anchored, blew up the dinghy, and rowed ashore.

We had the beach to ourselves. It was idyllic. Oystercatchers swooped round the bay. In the crystal-clear, unpolluted waters, sand eels wound their way over the seabed. Pete braved the cold and went for a swim. And when we went back to the boat, I cooked up a delicious chicken chasseur with broccoli and potatoes, followed by strawberries and yoghurt, washed down by wine we'd bought when we dropped off Tim in Ullapool, as the sun went down over the Atlantic and *Liberty* rocked gently in the bay.

And if I haven't yet persuaded you about the joys of sailing, I don't think I ever will.

oooOOOooo

Chapter 18

The Lofoten Wall

To me, the joys of sailing are inseparable from the joys of friendship. And though I have sailed with many friends, there are two who stand out above all others, and that's why this book is dedicated to them as well as to my children.

Howard Steen, my climbing partner on Tower Ridge back in 1972 and for five years afterwards until my MS diagnosis, has lived in Germany since 1988, but we still see each other as often as we can. I'd been trying to interest him in sailing for years, and in June 1988 I finally persuaded him to join me, Sally, my parents and a couple of their friends for a fortnight's holiday on a chartered yacht, *Highland Dream*, with me as designated skipper. I'm glad that he did. Good friends know everything about you. They know your parents, your family, what you're like to live with in close confines, and what sort of person you are even when you are pushed to your limits – like, for example, when you're on your first big winter climb on the north face of Ben Nevis.

Howard already knew all of that. But that trip, I now realise, deepened our friendship even further. Before, if I had talked about the joys of sailing, Howard mightn't have understood: he had never been on a boat for a day, never mind a fortnight. The plan was to sail through the most spectacular landscape in Britain, on a gentle 13-day cruise from Dunstaffnage, across the Minch to South Uist, and back round Skye and to Plockton and then Loch Hourn, one of the most spectacular lochs in Scotland. And it wasn't all plain sailing: off Knoydart, we found ourselves in the middle of a Royal Marines training exercise, and when we crossed the Minch from

Loch Scavaig, half the voyage was in fog. And in those pre-GPS days, this could be scary. Unless you were 100 per cent certain of your navigational abilities, you never knew what you were going to bump into.

When I look back, in fact, the weather on that trip was far from perfect. We started off in bright sunshine, but many days were overcast, dreich or changeable. Maybe (I can't remember, but it was Scotland in June, so it's an informed guess) there were midges. There were certainly plenty of things about that voyage – not least, having seven adults crammed together in a 34ft boat – that were hardly ideal.

If there were, Howard clearly saw beyond them. By the time we dropped him off at Plockton to catch the train home, he too had caught the sailing bug. So in 1991, when I was sitting my RYA yachtmaster exams in Glasgow and on the Clyde, he was sitting his coastal skipper exams alongside me. And soon after he retired in 2008, he bought *Martha Maria*. She was the sort of boat I'd have picked myself: a solid, safe, well-designed, Vancouver 27, a pocket-sized cruiser designed to cross oceans – indeed, her previous owners, who lived in Hamburg and kept her in the Baltic (or the Ostsee, as Germans call it), had sailed her all the way down to Rio and Cape Town.

Remember when I mentioned that sailing gave me the extra edge to life that I'd always found in climbing? Well, there's no better proof than the sailing trips Howard and I have made together.

Back in the mid-Seventies, the university mountaineering club to which we both belonged organised an expedition to the Lofoten Islands. Because of other commitments at the time, neither of us could join it, but we resolved that one day we would go there ourselves. The Lofoten Islands in Arctic Norway are, it must be said, among the most impressive climbing areas on the planet. The mountains there aren't particularly high – the highest, Higraftindan, is only 1,161m – but because they rise straight up from the sea, they are extraordinarily spectacular. The Norwegians call them the Lofoten Wall, and when you see them on the horizon, that is indeed what they look like – although their dramatic silhouette is actually more like shards of broken glass cemented into the top of a wall to deter burglars. We couldn't wait to climb those jagged Lofoten peaks, maybe in the summer, when we could do so in the midnight sun.

It never happened, of course: my MS got in the way. But when Howard's love affair with sailing began, another possibility presented itself. We couldn't climb the Lofoten Islands. But we could at least sail there.

Decades passed before we tried. Howard kept *Martha Maria* in the Baltic, and each year from 2009 to 2011, sailed her nearer and nearer to the Lofotens. I would join him for two or three weeks at a time. That first year, he sailed to Sweden and I joined him at the end of the season as we sailed along its southern coast. The next year, he sailed round the Norwegian coast to Bergen, and I helped out as he took *Martha Maria* to her sheltered winter berth afloat at Norheimsund, halfway down Hardangerfjord's longest side-fjord. I also spent a week on the boat that winter, and even did a little bit of skiing. The following year – 2011 – we made the big push north to the Lofotens.

I joined Howard and *Martha Maria* at a small port 80 miles north of Bergen and we set off. I had three weeks before I needed to return to my job at Salford Royal, and the Lofotens were 800 miles to the north. I wanted to make use of every minute.

As we sailed up the coast, the nights became increasingly short, the mountains bigger and creeping nearer the shore. At Engen, Howard nipped ashore, climbed up to the Svartisen glacier and brought back a thermos full of ice for our malt whiskies on the boat. For some obscure bureaucratic reason to do with exporting yachts, we had to sail *Martha Maria* outside Norwegian territorial waters for a while, so we plotted a course far enough out into the Norwegian Sea, took a picture of the GPS reading as evidence in case we were challenged, and pressed on northwards, sailing for up to 30 hours without a break. When we finally got there, even after 30 years' waiting to see them, the Lofoten Islands didn't disappoint.

In *The Hitchiker's Guide to the Galaxy*, written by Douglas Adams (who was the year below me both at Brentwood and at St John's), the designer of planets is called Slartibartfast. He's particularly proud of the Earth, and most especially of the intricate filigree work he did on the coast of Norway, and the Lofoten Islands are a classic example of this coastal complexity. They shelter the coast of northern Norway in the same way that the Outer Hebrides stand guard over the north-west coast of Scotland. But there the similarities end. The Lofoten Islands are an even more spectacular island chain, breathtaking and imposing even from a distance, when all that can be seen of them are the silhouettes of their peaks on the horizon. Graphs are like this, and so are children's ideas of mountains, but in real life we seldom see anything comparable, and certainly not powering up from the sea like an army of St Kildas, Borerays and Skellig Michaels all ominously massed together.

Up close, you start to see that the Lofoten Wall isn't actually a solid mass of land, and that the sea has frayed it away to make a chain of granite islands with occasional improbably steep-sided channels between them. Close-up, you can begin to make out village ports, with snowy peaks looming above them. Life here must have been as hard and as poor and almost as isolated as it ever was in St Kilda, yet now this once neglected land is part of the richest country in Europe. Those villages sheltering underneath mountains are neat, tidy, their rust-coloured paint freshly applied and not peeling away, the road between them, though long and extremely winding, impeccably maintained. As well as being awesome, these days the Lofotens are also prosperous.

As it was high summer when we reached them, there were no nights. At half past eleven one night we got out the dinghy and rowed away from the anchored *Martha Maria* so we could take photos of her in the midnight sun. There wasn't a whisper of wind, only the tiniest ripple on the surface of the water. In the photos we took, *Martha Maria* was bathed in a soft, golden light, with the mountains and islands all around. If I ever think of the world as a cruel, ugly place, that's a memory that will resurface to remind me that it's not.

I flew home from Bodø, well inside the Arctic Circle, but Howard moored *Martha Maria* even further north at Tromsø, a delightful university city and surprisingly cultured one. Tromsø calls itself "the Paris of the North", which may be pushing it a bit, but in fairness, it does have good art galleries and museums, an arts cinema and is home, along with Bodø, to Europe's most northerly orchestra.

In March 2012, I flew back to rejoin Howard on *Martha Maria*. The land of the midnight sun was now, for us, almost sunless: and in our sheltered and shadowy corner of the harbour the sun didn't rise above the harbour buildings until the end of the month. Snow fell intermittently, and sea ice occasionally began to form. But although the low winter sun provided some brilliantly clear (if short) days when we were ashore, the nights were spectacular.

The Northern Lights, of course. I had never seen them before. In 2009, I had joined a yacht as a paying passenger on the western coast of Greenland, and while that voyage had introduced me to the beautiful menace of icebergs and spectacular scenery, I had been far too late to catch a glimpse of the aurora borealis. In Tromsø, however, I was in the right place at the right time.

Howard became mildly obsessed with the Northern Lights. He could tell you all about the Norwegian scientist who was the first man to correctly explain what they actually were and demonstrated them in his laboratory. He even went off to the Tromsø library to search out the English language version of the 1907 book by Professor Kristian Birkeland in which he outlined his theories – dismissed by the British scientific establishment at the time – and when the library didn't have it, went off to track it down at Tromsø University's physics department library.

I didn't entirely share Howard's fascination with the Northern Lights, but I can understand it. First of all, those curtains of green light in the sky do indeed have their own otherworldly beauty. This is the reason that Tromsø in March is, as he pointed out, full of people lugging around camera tripods, which are essential for the long-exposure shots of the night sky that you need in order to be able to capture an image of the northern lights that bears any resemblance to what you can see with your own eyes. But there is another reason I find the Northern Lights inspiring, and it's nothing to do with their appearance and everything to do with what they are.

In 1902, Birkeland proposed that the Northern Lights were essentially caused by electrons, emitted from the sun as a result of solar flares, hitting the Earth's geomagnetic field. Nonsense, said the other "experts": how could anything possibly cross the vacuum of space – clearly, this was a phenomenon generated entirely within our planet. Fifty years after his death, however, Birkeland was vindicated. A US satellite carrying a magnetometer over the ionosphere proved the existence of electric currents flowing along geomagnetic field lines just as he had predicted.

Step back from the detail of the science, though, and look at the big picture. Those solar winds that take just eight minutes to arrive here from the sun have blasted away the atmospheres in the rest of our neighbouring planets. Without Earth's magnetic poles holding onto it, our atmosphere too would vanish, leaving our planet just as dead as Mars. Those lights dancing above my head in the ionosphere are charged particles from the sun releasing energy as they meet the Earth's magnetic shield. In a sense, they're a sign that our planet is fighting back. Yes, they are pretty. Yes, they are visually awe-inspiring. But the greater awe is when you look on the Northern Lights as being more than that. They are a reminder of the fragility of life itself. Without these magnetic disturbances and their strangely beautiful manifestations in the skies above me, there would be no atmosphere, no life, no fish in the oceans, no animals on the land, no leaves on the trees, no trees, no plants even. No me, no you, no us. The Arctic air is clear, unpolluted. You can see miles further there. But when you look at the Northern Lights blowing above you like luminous light green misty washing, what you are seeing is the reason Earth is not an empty, desiccated, lifeless planet. You are looking at the reason everything you've loved about today will still be around tomorrow. You are looking at a normally invisible force that allows life to exist.

Howard understood that long before I did, although these days I probably think about it even more than him.

The Northern Lights may well have been the highlight of that March trip to Norway, and we saw them again from the Hurtigruten ferry on the five-hour crossing from Skjervøy to Tromsø. Away from the bright lights of the big city (and with a 65,000 population, Tromsø *is* a big city in Arctic terms) the aurora shone even brighter. There were plenty of other highlights from my time in Norway. Skiing across the frozen Prestvannet Lake. Sailing south again, with a fine northerly in our sails, after I rejoined *Martha Maria* at Bodø for nine days in June. Fine though they were, they were nothing compared to our first sight of the Lofoten Islands. It's not given to everyone to achieve major ambitions, much less one that took the best past of four decades.

It's a sign of the depth of the friendship Howard and I have for each other that he persisted in helping me to reach the Lofotens after all those years. That friendship, formed four and a half decades ago on a Scottish mountain, has never faltered. And through it, he has helped me fulfil another ambition too.

We have been going to the Kendal Mountain Festival most years since 1993. For anyone who loves the outdoors, adventure, climbing and photography it's an unmissable event, and the film festival at its heart is widely regarded as the "Oscars of outdoor film-making." One year – I forget which – I had the bright idea that we should make a film about sailing and enter the competition ourselves. The fact that neither of us knew anything about film-making wouldn't hold us back: the festival ran courses expressly for novices like us.

It never happened. Howard loves photography but, in that pre-digital age, film editing looked off-puttingly time-consuming. In April 2014, however, he met a film-making enthusiast who offered to shoot a film for us in exchange for crewing on *Martha Maria*. Fine: but what would the story be?

I remember one day getting a phone call from Howard. How, he asked, would I feel about the film focussing on my struggle with MS and the way in which sailing provided me with a sense of adventure that might otherwise have been lost when I was forced to quit climbing? He was, I could tell, embarrassed to be asking the question. He knows full well how much I loathe being defined by my disease – the very reason, for example, behind what some might see as my stubborn refusal to use a blue badge disability parking badge on my car. Yet here he was asking if I wouldn't mind making a whole film in which the way I dealt with my MS would be central. I could sense his relief when I agreed that it would be a good idea; the fact is, I had been thinking along similar lines myself. We'd make the film in August that year, we all agreed.[23] Howard would sail up to the Cuillin Mountains in Skye with the film-maker in *Martha Maria*; Peter and I would turn up in *Liberty*. The film would be about me attempting to reach the foot of the Dubhs Ridge, above Loch Coruisk, which I climbed back in my Cambridge days in 1971, as I described in Chapter 4. We would shoot some more footage in 2015 and enter it for the Kendal festival by its September deadline.

Things didn't work out as planned with our film-making friend, and we never made that deadline. But we did at least agree that both he and Howard could each use the (admittedly excellent) footage they had already shot. Howard realised that if the project was ever going to happen, he would have to master the art of film editing. A Dutch-American film-maker called Guus Floor came on board to help with the storytelling, tighten the narration, improve the music, and speed up its pace. This is the film that we now have. It's called *Revisiting the Dubhs Ridge*, and you can see it for free on the internet if you type the title into your search engine.[24] We're all proud of it and it has just been recognized with an 'Exceptional Merit' award from a large US Documentary Film Festival.

People who have watched the film say that one of the things they find most moving about it is its straightforward depiction of friendship. They're right. Of course, I never tell them this, but I have some of the best friends in the world.

oooOOOooo

---

23 Sadly my father died in August 2014, just before we were due to start filming, which delayed the project by several weeks.
24 See – https://vimeo.com/215021897

Chapter 19

The Lounge in Lerwick

Pete reckons it must have been the summer of 1960, and that sounds about right to me. Our fathers had been friends ever since working together at Metro Vicks towards the end of the Second World War, and they probably hoped that we would be too. All I can remember is the Davies' family car pulling up at Clegir, and playing at tunnelling through the bracken at the front of the cottage with their son who, like me, was eight.

Ten years pass, and Pete and I are at Cambridge together, sons of engineers, both studying engineering and both not really enjoying it. Our parents hoped we would be friends, and we were. Almost fifty years have passed, and we still are.

How does a lifelong friendship start? Is there anything genetic to it – or is it a completely random, spur-of-the-moment thing? Howard's father, Pete's and mine were all passionate about engineering: were their sons somehow predisposed to like each other? Was it all a matter of shared memories of Cambridge as we grew older? Was it because we all loved the outdoors? Is friendship just a matter of accumulating shared experience – or is there anything more to it than that?

In *The Four Loves*, CS Lewis gives as good an answer as I can find. "Friendship," he wrote, "is born at that moment when one person says to the other 'What! You too? I thought I was the only one.'"

With Howard, that moment happened when we met at the CIC Hut on Ben Nevis in April 1972 and realised just how much we had in common. With Pete, perhaps because I have known him for even longer, I cannot identify any single friendship-starting moment. Instead, it grew over the years, from something begun almost out of a sense of filial obligation to something far more than that. We didn't just have our ambivalent attitude to engineering in common (or, ultimately, careers that took us both to jobs in the field of health); it was the love of outdoors, too. Maybe it was a brief walking trip with Pete to the Mer de Glace in Chamonix in August 1971 that made the difference. It was only a two-day break from an unpaid internship I was doing in Geneva, but it was the first time I'd seen Mont Blanc. I knew those Alpine peaks were far higher than any mountains we had in Britain, but until then, I had absolutely no idea what that actually meant. Even though Pete and I walked on relatively easy paths above the tree line, I couldn't stop marvelling at how immensely high those snowy peaks rose above us. I was transfixed. The next year I was climbing some of them.

Whatever the roots of our friendship, it has nothing to do with climbing, snowy peaks or otherwise. It only took Pete one day's climbing with me – the Yellow Groove VS route on Craig Du in the Llanberis Pass – to decide against any further rock face adventures. At one stage, on our first sail together, I thought Pete had turned against sailing too. In April 1992, I chartered a yacht at Ullapool – a Rival 38 called *Anitra* – and invited Howard and Pete along as crew. Howard was already quite committed to sailing, having passed his RYA coastal skipper exam the previous year, but I wasn't sure about Pete. I knew he had sailed Flying 15s and Flying Junior dinghies in his teens, but when we were out in the middle of the Minch, heading for Loch Laxford, just south of Cape Wrath, he was repeatedly seasick and shivering with cold. But I needn't have worried: at the same time, almost perversely, he felt the same sense of exhilaration that I find in sailing too – that joy in timelessness, in losing oneself in the sea's enormity while at the same time trying to master its unpredictability.

That week-long trip sealed Pete's love of offshore sailing. Since then, we have sailed together every year. He likes to say that he's the brawn and I'm the brains in the partnership, that he's better at leaping onto jetties or pulling up the anchor and I'm better at charting a course clear of reefs and rocks. This may well be true, but what matters more to me is that it's a partnership that works. It's one that has deepened over the years too. He was devastated when his marriage collapsed in 1997. "Come on, Pete," I said, "let's go sailing." Off we went for a week dotting around the Inner Hebrides, and the therapeutic balm of salty breezes, spectacular scenery, and the joys of both sailing and friendship helped ease the pain. Our voyages together got longer as we grew older (especially after I bought *Minella* and Pete bought into *Liberty*), and as I drifted towards semi-retirement and Pete actually did retire from his job as Dean of School at the University of Westminster. Finally, we had the long stretches of time – six weeks, say – we needed for the kind of voyages we really wanted to make.

Of them all, I'll just pick one. Howard sailed west across the Norwegian Sea from Bergen to Lerwick; Pete and I sailed north to Shetland to meet him. All easily said; all not so easily done, in the second half of May and the whole of June 2013.

For a start, the winds were against us. We set off from Bangor determined to sail round Cape Wrath – the north-west tip of the Scottish mainland – and cross seas I had never sailed in my life. But the winds weren't co-operating. Gales blew in from the north, forcing us to stay in port for longer than we wanted, first of all at *Liberty*'s home base of Port Dinorwic near Bangor, then again at Port St Mary in the Isle of Man. When we did finally get a move on, after reaching Scotland, there was another delay. And this time it wasn't the wind's fault.

We were half-way through the Sound of Luing, which is roughly halfway between Ardlussa on Jura and Oban on a part of the Argyll coast that, on the map, looks like a pile of dropped slates. The winds, forecast as light to moderate, turned out to be Force 7, which normally wouldn't have been a problem at all. Except now they were, because the forestay – an 8mm wire from the top of the mast to the front of the boat – suddenly snapped. This was serious, the way a snapped brake cable in a car is serious: wind in the sails of a mast that is not properly secured could easily bring it toppling down. In pounding seas, we got the sails down as fast as we could, and Pete crawled on his hands and knees across the deck up to the pulpit (the railing at the front of the boat) and managed to lash up a temporary replacement forestay to make everything secure. We motored into Kerrara and waited, for four days, for the gales to blow over and the repairs to finish, before heading north again.

South Rona, Tanera Beg, Lochinver, Kinlochbervie: these were all well-known to Pete and me, welcome checkpoints on voyages north. But round Cape Wrath, the seas off the north coast of Scotland were new to us both, as we headed for, and then explored, the Orkney Islands. We'd been advised against pushing on to Shetland, but the weather forecast promised near-perfect conditions, and we sailed from Westray (one of the more northerly Orkney Islands) to Scalloway, halfway up the west coast of Shetland, on a single tack – 74 miles in 12 hours.

And that, essentially, was the story we had to tell Howard when we finally met him. He had sailed *Martha Maria* from Norway to Lerwick, on the east coast of Shetland, and we met him there. He then sailed counter-clockwise to Scalloway[25], we sailed Liberty clockwise round to Lerwick. Our boats met in the Sound of Yell, to the north, and we passed near enough each other for us to shout greetings and take photos. But it is our third Shetland meeting that sticks in my mind the longest. We were by now moored in Lerwick, and Howard (joined by James) in Scalloway, but they came over to us by taxi. While they were in Lerwick earlier, they had discovered a pub they liked called The Lounge.

You'd miss it easily enough. There's a door in a building sticking out apologetically into the pavement on Mounthooly Street, with a weather-beaten, broken-lettered sign above its door in white-trimmed red letters in a 1950s font that nobody uses any more. At night, a small spotlight comes on, but it's angled to the left, so all it clearly says is "THE LOU". It's one of those pubs that's not

25 Where anyone sailing (as Howard had done) from Norway – or indeed anyone interested in the Second World War – should check out the excellent Scalloway Museum exhibition on the "Shetland Bus" network delivering secret agents and supplies between the Shetland Islands and Nazi-occupied Norway.

much to look at, but its regulars are as friendly as you'll meet anywhere – in fact, because Shetland is so relatively remote, they make more of a fuss about strangers. So it's a welcoming place, there's a good selection of beers and whiskies, and if you go on a Wednesday or Saturday night and head upstairs, you'll hear some of the best folk music in Scotland. Shetland fiddle music – fearsomely fast-paced and with distinctive bowing patterns – is wonderful, and from 10 o'clock for at least three hours, the room spun with reels, jigs and occasional slow airs. I found myself talking to one of the fiddlers, whose mother turned out to have once been a dedicated MS nurse. When I told her that I had the disease too, and how far we'd come on this voyage, she could hardly believe it.

On nights like that one at The Lounge in Lerwick, life is at its best. You go somewhere you don't know is going to be wonderful, but it turns out to be. You meet friends you haven't seen for far too long, tell them about your own adventures en route and listen to their own stories. You meet new friends – the next day, back at the harbour, we met a man circumnavigating the UK and running 10K at ten different ports, all for charity – and between sips of Talisker and Jura on board in *Liberty* you get a sense of what their lives are like too. But it's your own friends that mean the most, and right there round the table in The Lounge, were some of the very best of mine: Howard, who had first come offshore sailing with me in 1988; James, a *Martha Maria* regular with whom I had been on many voyages; and Pete, with whom I'd been friends for the longest of all, and whom I had also introduced to the joys of offshore sailing.

There's someone else I should mention, another friend of *Liberty*, and someone else who enjoyed his adventures on it. Sadly, the previous year, our good friend Tim Jeans, a successful aviation entrepreneur, made the last of his many voyages on *Liberty*. In an appalling coincidence, in 2010 he was diagnosed with MS too and by 2012 he felt he had better give up sailing. I'd known him since 2003, when our daughters became friends, and we still 'phone each other practically every week. The disease we have in common makes us reassess our daily goals. As he points out, each day is a matter of "small wins"; if you can put your socks on at the first attempt, for example, that's one, because an unsuccessful effort might leave you too exhausted to try again for hours. If you can get your legs through your trousers, that's another "small win".

I knew that those small wins get harder as secondary progressive MS took its hold, so it was all the more important to make the most of the "big wins" of friendship, and to celebrate a night like this. That's why, even though Howard and James and Peter and I had our separate adventures when we split up and went back to our home ports, it's this furthest northern evening in a pub that sticks longest in the memory and why I'll end this part of the story there. Because The Lounge in Lerwick, was in a sense, where we'd all been aiming for, even if we didn't know it when we set off. A place that is now engraved on all of our own internal maps, somewhere firmly anchored in our minds when we think of friendship.

oooOOOooo

Of all the anchorages in the Summer Isles, the one we like best is the sheltered channel between the two uninhabited islets of Tanera Beg and Eilean Fada Mor. To the east, the porcupine ridges of Stac Pollaidh stand guard over the surrounding land like a colossal fortress, to the west the setting sun over the Outer Hebrides turns the Torridon sandstone cliffs even pinker. All this and coral sands, occasional otters, wild flowers growing in profusion in the absence of grazing sheep, and the remote coastal villages of Wester Ross within easy striking distance: it's no wonder that it had become a favourite.

Pete and I had anchored there on our 2013 voyage north to meet up with Howard and *Martha Maria* in Shetland; and on 24 May 2015 we headed there again. This time, we were shooting more footage for *Revisiting the Dubhs Ridge*. For the film, we used the two yachts, *Martha Maria*, and *Liberty*, which by now was jointly owned by Pete and myself. We all met at Tobermory, where I filmed some scenes talking about MS and at the chart table, and then we sailed north, anchoring overnight at Muck, Mallaig, Loch Duich and, on 23 May, that other firm favourite of ours, South Rona. The next day, Sunday 24 May, was one of those magical days on which I'd defy anyone not to enjoy sailing: a beam reach north to Rubha Reidh and then downwind to Tanera Beg in the Summer Isles: 40 glorious miles and in a mere seven hours.

We did a bit more filming and recording while anchored in Tanera Beg then in our two yachts sailed up Loch Broom to Ullapool. Howard needed to wait there for his Edinburgh friend James to arrive but Pete and I decided to continue north so we sailed back to Tanera Beg and anchored there for the night. I made supper and we each went off to bed. And that's when the drama began.

At 11:30pm, I heard Pete retching in the loo. He was in agony, clutching his stomach and grimacing with the pain, which seemed to come in 20-minute waves, ranging from just about bearable to what he said was the worst pain he'd ever felt. The first thing to do was to check for peritonitis: if Pete's gut had somehow been perforated, I'd have to somehow summon a helicopter, as he could be dead within hours. Except, look where we were. The anchorage at Tanera Beg was indeed sheltered, but the island sheltering us also blocked out the VHF radio. We couldn't get any mobile phone reception either. We were on our own.

The fact that the pain was coming in crescendos, however, was good news, although it wouldn't have seemed like that at the time to Pete. Pain in waves indicated a colicky pain rather than a chronic one, and because it was to one side and radiating towards the groin, I thought it must be renal colic. A kidney stone. That couldn't kill Pete, but it would produce an immense amount of pain. We had to get Pete to hospital – urgently.

He had already, with superhuman effort, raised the anchor, and had gone back down to the cabin to try to rest. At about three o'clock in the morning, in pitch darkness, we set off for Ullapool, nosing gently out of our anchorage. Until we reached open sea, the course we had to chart was particularly tricky: we had to keep within 25 yards of a cliff on the starboard side while avoiding some hidden rocks off to port. We had three things going for us. First, when we got out to sea, the wind was in our favour. Secondly, we had GPS. Thirdly, and probably most importantly, we had our friend Bob Bradfield's large-scale Antares chart for Tanera Beg, showing with perfect accuracy just where the rocks were, and how deep the channels were between them.

At the best of times, there aren't too many lights on this part of the Scottish coast. At three o'clock in the morning, I couldn't see a single one. The rocks, the cliffs, and the shallows were all hidden in the pitch darkness. Without Bob's chart on our iPad, getting out to the open sea would have been fraught with danger.

Once out of the radio shadow of Tanera Beg, I managed to get through to the coastguard, who arranged for an ambulance to meet *Liberty* at the pontoon in Ullapool at 7am, Thursday morning. But the passage there was positively Wagnerian. As Pete battled pain in the cabin, hailstones rattled down on the deck above. Four hours later, though, we were there. Pete managed to tie off the mooring lines, and staggered off the pontoon towards the ambulance, where morphine and Endotox kept the pain at bay on the 90-minute dash to hospital in Inverness. There, they tested him for diverticulitis and pancreatitis, but his X-rays and blood tests were both fine. Only then, and after another pain attack, did they test for a kidney stone and give him the abdominal CT scan I had suggested. This confirmed that Pete did indeed have a kidney stone, and he had a successful operation to remove it the following night (Friday). I was glad to see the old Chisholm diagnostic skills hadn't gone rusty. I was even gladder to see Pete walking along the jetty at Gairloch to rejoin *Liberty* three nights later.

One last thing before I finish this chapter. Although ostensibly it's about sailing to Shetland, really it's all been about friendship. That friendship has been based on our times sailing together, but it works on dry land too. I never saw it more clearly than this summer.

For 13 weekends in succession, Pete came up to see me as I struggled to cope with the virulent disease I'll describe in the next chapter. Each time, it was a long and tiresome train journey or drive from London up to Manchester or Holyhead. I owe Jane, his partner for the last 10 years, a great debt of gratitude for her forbearance. But I owe Pete, for his lifelong friendship, more than I can say.

oooOOOooo

Chapter 20

Two Short Straws

I've always used toeclips when I cycle. For people with MS, they're particularly useful, keeping your feet exactly where they should be on the pedals. It can be a bit exasperating when you can't get your feet into them, but once they're in, they're in.

At the start of 2017, though, I noticed something new. In all the years I've cycled with MS – almost four decades – I'd never had any trouble getting my feet *out* of the toeclips. Yet now I did. One day, as I cycled home from work, I managed to fall off my bike twice within ten yards of my front door. I tried not to worry about it: I had been walking a lot around the hospital at work, and maybe my legs were just more tired than usual. But my falls were becoming more frequent, even on the 15-minute cycle ride to work. I had cycled that route almost every working day since 1989, and this had never happened before. For the first time, I thought I had better arrange a disabled parking space outside the ultrasound department at the hospital.

I was annoyed at having to admit defeat like this, but there was worse to come. One day, I found that my left leg was becoming so weak that I could no longer even lift it to the pedals. This, I reckoned, must be another sign of secondary progressive MS – the stage the disease reaches when relapses stop and gradual deterioration begins – that I'd been told to expect five years previously. I was also becoming increasingly depressed, but I reckoned that was probably MS-related too. If you had spent your life trying to defy a disease and it was tightening its grip on you despite everything you did, depression seemed an entirely natural reaction.

There is one advantage of working in a hospital that is the neurology centre for all of Greater Manchester, and it's that you don't have to go far to find specialised expertise. I mentioned my worries to a lovely man called Mark Kellett, the clinical director of the city's Neurosciences Centre. "Just to be sure, you should have an MRI scan," he said.

At five o'clock that same day, a patient hadn't turned up for their appointment, so there was a free slot. I assumed the position on the scanner bed, everything was made ready, and off I moved into the machine, which stopped just before my shoulders, and slid back again for repeated scans.

The following morning, while I was reporting chest CT scans in my office, Amit Herwadkar, one of my neuroradiological colleagues, came in to see me. I'd known Amit for years. I trained him as a registrar and had been on the appointments committee 18 years previously when he had been made a consultant. He, too, is a lovely, sensitive man.

"Amit," I said, "is there a cause for my weak left leg?"

He nodded. There were tears in his eyes.

He showed me the contrast enhanced images and discussed the diagnostic possibilities with me.

What was most likely, he said, was that I had an aggressive brain tumour. A less likely possibility was that the tumour was a metastasis from a tumour elsewhere in my body. Least likely of all was what is called a tumorfactive demyelination, which basically means a pseudo-tumour related to MS. It didn't really look like one, but because of my 40-year history of MS, they wanted to be absolutely certain. This was my best bet, as it was the only option that was easily treatable.

I saw my brain surgeon the next day, and she agreed to operate in five days' time. Tissue would be taken from the affected part of my brain and examined by the neuropathologists to determine whether or not it was – as my surgeon suspected – a malignant tumour.

Sally had been with me at that meeting, and she subsequently took control of the situation. She is a great organiser, practical and efficient. She broke the news to Elinor and Owen and the close friends and family who needed to know. For those five days, she made sure that I didn't have to do a thing.

And I didn't, apart from worry. My mind raced around all the possibilities of what my life would be like after the operation. First of all, how much of it would there be? Days? Months? Years? As you have probably already worked out, I am the kind of person who likes to set a goal and then work towards it. Climbing was like that, so too was sailing, and so, I suppose, was my whole career.

But this was different. This was like setting out on a tightrope walk over a chasm where you couldn't see the other end, and where the rope could be cut at any time. The walk itself would be terrifying enough, but if the rope could be cut at any time, what was the point even setting out on it in the first place? How could you begin to plan anything? How could you ever remain in control of your own life? And if you weren't, what was the point of it?

Like any man my age – I was 65 – I had lost far too many dear friends who had died far too young. Like any doctor, I had seen death up close. Every day at work, the scans I looked at didn't only, for all our best efforts, chart a course towards health and recovery: many were also markers on the path to death. But in those five days, thoughts about death weren't the only ones spinning into my flywheel mind. Brain operations could easily go wrong. Remove too much of the tumour, slice off a millimetre or so of working, thinking tissue, and what then? My mind, still working frighteningly well and imaginatively, threw up all possible variants of a bleak future. Wheelchair-bound, incontinent, babbling versions of myself stared back in my mind's eye. Perhaps I would be aphasic, incapable of doing anything useful. The prospect horrified me. Granted, it would horrify anyone, but I think my years of MS made it even worse.

Why? Because in all of them, the one thing I had avoided was what a brain tumour threatened to remove: I had avoided being dependent or being defined by the disease, often so successfully that people didn't realise I had it. Wherever possible I didn't walk with a stick, nor until 2017 did I apply for the blue badge as a disabled driver even though I had been entitled to one for decades. This wasn't vanity; it was fundamental. My whole personality leads me to seek out and live a life of freedom, friendship and, to the extent allowed me, adventure. Judge a man by what's on his screensaver: Half-Dome, the huge granite cliff in Yosemite, one of the great free-climbing challenges. That's the direction in which my mind works, even if my body no longer does.

I had fought and fought to make my own way in life despite MS, to use my brain and lead a useful life. But however the operation worked out, it was going to bring down the shutters on the kind of independent life I wanted to lead. Friends, then and now, counselled acceptance. That's easy to say, and doubtless wise. But I was in no mood for acceptance, nor could I will myself into it, the way I had willed myself to achieve so many other things.

Those five days didn't take long to pass, and after a night in which my mind bubbled over with thoughts of the future, I got up early and was in surgical admissions at 5am. Oddly enough, given that I've spent most of my life in hospitals, I'd never had anaesthetic or an operation in one: indeed, I'd only ever spent one night in a hospital as a patient in my life – back in Cambridge, during a particularly bad phase of MS. Still, I knew what to expect. A brief chat with the junior doctor. Then the consultant anaesthetist. Then the surgeon. The needle in my arm and the loss of consciousness.

I woke up in theatre recovery a few hours later. The anaesthetist was talking to me. It was indeed a malignant tumour, he said. They'd done the tests and taken out – *debulked*, to use the correct terminology – as much of it as they safely could.

What he didn't spell out then – but what I knew was true – was that some of the tumour was left in my brain, that it would grow back, and that it would kill me.

Before I sank back to sleep, I did a quick bit of mental arithmetic in my head to see whether my brain was working. Seven times eight was, mercifully, still fifty-six.

oooOOOooo

It's six months later and I am sitting writing this in an end of life nursing home near Holyhead. They've given me a room on the top floor because they know how much the sea means to me and I have a great view of it from up here. Since July I've been able to watch the dinghies flutter about in the bay half a mile away.

I'm here because it's where my cousin Rosemary works. She's one of the most caring people I know; 73, and still looking after old crocks like me out of the boundless goodness of her heart. She's so cheery that I always look forward to seeing her. She knows I'm working on this book, and the other day she asked me what I was going to call it. I said I didn't know. "Have *you* any ideas?" I asked.

"You could always call it *Tits Up*," she said.

Well, it made me laugh anyway.

I know how books like this are supposed to end. There's usually something about the circularity of life and acceptance of death. I could easily, if only it were completely true, wrap up this story like that. After all, here's cousin Rosemary coming into my room to cheer me up, and she's still the same warm-hearted, kind person I remember from my childhood when we were at Clegir and they were a mile away across the valley. And those dinghies scudding about in the late September breeze? They're not too different from the ones we were always capsizing as teenagers on the Menai Straits on the other side of Anglesey. That Irish Sea I often catch myself looking wistfully across at is the same sea my father sailed us across in 1969, as my own love of sailing began to grow inside me like, well, whatever the opposite of cancer is.

All of that is true, but it's not the whole story, and if you can't tell the whole story when you're facing up to death, what's the point in telling your story at all?

When, six months ago, in my still-drugged state, I heard the anaesthetist confirm that I did indeed have a malignant brain tumour, I closed my eyes in despair and dropped off back to oblivion. Deep down, although my mind was still whirring through all kinds of different potential futures, the thing I felt most was a primal sense of unfairness. All those years of multiple sclerosis – four whole decades, almost – and now this? Forty years of building a career, of saving up for a retirement in which I could spend more time with my children, sailing with friends or at the cottage at Snowdonia – and now what? All those years of trying not to be defined by disease and – bang – here comes another one right on top of it, one that there was just no way round, even if I tried.

Taking back control. That's what the politicians have been going on about for the last couple of years. I'm not bothered about Brexit, but I would love to take back control of my own life and I am bitter about the fact that I can't. Friends and family have, I know, come away from visiting me shocked at how angry I was, how much I wanted to commit suicide. At least if I did that, I thought, I would be taking back control. I wouldn't just be waiting anxiously for the tightrope to nowhere to be cut: at least I would be in charge of my own death, just as I had been of my life.

Back in May 2017, as I began 30 solid days of radiotherapy and chemotherapy, I felt less in control of my life than I ever had been. My mind was racing through a succession of different but usually equally horrible futures, and at the same time the treatment schedule was piling up. I was a cork borne along on the terminal illness river: every day for 30 days I had to be at the Christie Hospital in Manchester as the treatment got underway. If I didn't have any, they told me, I'd be dead in six months (which is precisely the time at which I am writing this); if I did, well, who can say? Twelve months? Eighteen? There are some cases the oncologists can't explain where the patient might even live for another five years. We all hang on to the hope implicit in "miracle" cases like that, even rational scientists who should know better, who know the odds and who never gamble.

So the "miracle cure" scenario went into my mental mix too, but it never really stuck on the churning list of possible futures: I'm too much of a realist for that. Besides, my legs were getting weaker, whether through the chemo or not I didn't know, and I was feeling increasingly tired. Tired, and yet also rushed and out of control on the treatment superhighway. If only I could have stilled my mind – or if only there had been time to somehow pull off the treatment superhighway, maybe for counselling, maybe for a longer explanation of what my future held in store – I could have felt as though I was more in control.

By contrast to all of this, suicide did seem the more straightforward option. It was, I read, in brain surgeon Henry Marsh's excellent memoir *Do No Harm*, the one that he himself would choose if he were ever diagnosed with a brain tumour[26]. Besides, my life *was* a living hell, and I didn't believe in an afterlife, so suicide was an entirely logical option. Some people couldn't understand this. I had been so resilient in the way in which I had dealt with MS, they'd say: why couldn't I be like that now? Why couldn't I let go of the anger I felt? Why couldn't I stop feeling bitter at my fate? Why couldn't I make peace with the world?

Against that, there are moments when I don't feel like this at all. Friends come round and take me out for lunch. We laugh and remember and life is good again. I do love my children more than my own life, I am enormously proud of them both, and know how much they would be hurt by my suicide. I remember how much of a toll my sister Di's death took on my father. They don't need that.

And there's something else too. Something I realised even at my most profound moments of despair.

It's this. I have, despite 40 years of MS and a brain tumour, had a good life. Looking back on it, as I have been doing while writing this book, I realise that I have even been lucky.

I may not be able to go into wild places any more, but I will always have the memory of how much at home I felt there. The world has given me so many moments of happiness. Think of what you feel about the beauty of this planet when you watch a heron fishing on flat calm water. When you sail into a Scottish loch and see seals flopping into the water all around you. When you moor a

---

26 Although when a friend asked him whether he still stood by that, he said he wouldn't know for sure until the last moment and even then he wasn't sure whether his "suicide kit" would do the job.

boat and look down through crystal-clear water at anemones and crabs scuttling over white shell sand. Or when you're on the hills, sitting down on a heathery slope when you've climbed a thousand feet or so, and you're looking up and working out how much further there is to go, and you can feel the wind sighing against your face or hear the skylark singing its heart out.

And those are just the bedrock memories of what the wild places have meant. Whatever happens in my brain's right temporal lobe, it knows that I have also seen icebergs off Greenland and sailed under the Arctic sun in Norway, that I have walked 145 miles around Annapurna and taken the high roads of Waziristan, and clambered up an Austrian alpine pass with only one of my four limbs working properly. And because memories are not stored in one distinct part of the brain, my right temporal lobe will know, as a matter of course, that I did all of this while having MS.

Whilst writing this book, I have fired up all those memory neurons all over again, reinforcing the synaptic connections in the neural network. The more we think about past memories, it seems, the stronger those memories remain in our brain.

And what memories would I want to leap across my brain's synapses when the end inevitably comes and I slide off towards oblivion? There will be no shortage. As well as all my golden memories of Elinor and Owen, I think I will imagine being in a safe harbour with good friends. Peter will have dropped anchor, Howard will be cooking a meal, I'll be uncorking a bottle of red. We'll all be in Village Bay, St Kilda, and if it's not too much to ask, I'd also like to see the sea-stacks silhouetted in the evening sun.

So many memories. So much life. So much retrospective fondness for everyone I met in mine.

And maybe, at the end, I will even imagine myself into a memory my darling mother left behind when it was her turn to die.

It's the closing lines of a poem she wrote about our cottage in North Wales.

Two Short Straws

The afternoon drifts by
Too fast and the air turns cool. My daughter moves with her books
Out from the lengthening shadow. My husband stirs
From a sunny doze and his feet crackle under dead bracken.
It is time to make tea, while the radio is promising
Another lovely day tomorrow

oooOOOooo

Acknowledgements

There is a long list of people whose friendship, support and love I have valued and appreciated over the years, many of whom appear in this book. I am sure there will be some who I have failed to mention either below or in the book. If you are one of them, then please accept my apologies.

My years in Cambridge were some of my happiest, working alongside Tom Sherwood, Chris Flower, Alan Freeman, John Tudor also Pat Farman. In Manchester, I am particularly grateful to Hari Mamtora for his advice and companionship over the last 25 years; Anna Sharman and Anna Walsham for our time working together; Sarah Jackson and Dave Hughes for their support through difficult times and for delicious meals eaten whilst sitting in their gardens as respite from being in hospital during a long hot summer; Jill Carlin for being a great Clinical Director and friend over many years; Ronan O'Driscoll for being the best clinical colleague a radiologist could have for almost 30 years; Gillian Potter, I will always miss our Tuesday lunch time meetings; and where would I have been without Margaret Hawke and Julie Loughran, my dedicated secretaries over many years.

Good neighbours can be hard to come by and I have been particularly blessed in having Mary and Brennan Wilson nearby. Their friendship and support over more than 30 years are beyond measure, likewise that of Liz and Dave Yeates – not forgetting their respective families. In North Wales, Geoff Taylor couldn't have been a nicer neighbour. Marie Tyrrell, while not a neighbour has sometimes felt like one – a more dedicated GP you couldn't find.

Where would I be without friends? Sue Rees and Louise Holland have been steadfast in their friendship over the years, keeping in touch and more recently coming to visit. There are a great many other friends I would like to mention, but the friendship over the years of Tim Jeans, James Jack, Graham and Catherine Hurst, Ian and Fiona Martin, Tim and Ceri Dornan, Martin Steer, Rob Woodall, Derek and Anne Kite, Christina Shewell and Mark Vaughan I have appreciated especially. More recently, I am grateful for the love and friendship of Siobhan Davenport.

I am extremely grateful to Dr Rao and his dedicated oncology team at the Christie Hospital in Manchester, for making it possible for me to complete this project. Also to the very dedicated and caring staff at The Fairways Nursing Home in Anglesey, my cousin Rosemary Williams in particular. They have been absolutely wonderful and helped my recovery from my surgery and treatment over the past six months. I must also thank Sally Chisholm for her on-going support during this time.

Last but not least I extremely grateful to David Robinson for his invaluable and very sensitive help in seeing this book written, also to my good friend Bob Bradfield for responding so quickly to my query, shortly after I was diagnosed, about how a book like this might be written and for making the project possible. It has helped make the last six months bearable and worthwhile.

23rd October 2017

Afterword

This book was written over a six month period immediately after major brain surgery and during multiple courses of ongoing chemotherapy. Therefore, any deficiencies in the writing are probably due to my treatment rather than a lack of determination to describe the full and adventurous life that I have had.